The Zoning Game

The
Zoning
Game

Municipal Practices and Policies

RICHARD F. BABCOCK

The University of Wisconsin Press
Madison, Milwaukee, and London, 1966

Published by
The University of Wisconsin Press
Madison, Milwaukee, and London

U.S.A.: Box 1379, Madison, Wisconsin 53701
U.K.: 26–28 Hallam Street, London W.1

Library of Congress Catalog Card Number 66–22864

To Fred Bosselman and Jack Noble,
without whose inestimable help,
professional and personal, this
book would have been published
long ago.

Foreword

PERSONS who have had experience with zoning are rarely neutral about it. Ordinary citizens become rabid partisans, either pro or con. The planner for whom the zoning game is, more often than not, a primary occupation, if not a preoccupation, usually detests it, as Dick Babcock points out. This is especially true if the planner is one of the younger, or simulation-model, social-milieu, spatial-manipulation brand. How can you possibly get steamed up about whether a beauty shop is a customary home occupation when there is so much to be talked about on the choice theory as related to inter-group dynamics and calculated human intervention in normative social processes?

But for its devotees, the fascination of the zoning game never ends. The fascination of bridge as a game lies in the enormous number of possible permutations of the cards, so that although the number of different hands is finite, each new deal seems different and is quite unlikely to be exactly repeated during the player's lifetime.

The number of permutations in zoning problems may also be finite, but it is a number of a much greater magnitude than can be obtained with fifty-two playing cards dealt among four hands. Bridge or chess or any other such game is played everywhere with the same set of rules. The rules may change slightly over the years, but basically they remain constant and at any given time they are universally uniform. Not so with the zoning game. And this adds the extra fillip of interest that conventional games lack. Zoning might be likened to a great national bridge tournament, with 3,000 games going on at the same time, and with each foursome playing under its own set of rules. In fact, the opposing pairs at each table might use different rules.

The literature of zoning is not very extensive. After all, it is quite young, as human institutions go. In 1966 comprehensive zoning celebrates only its fiftieth anniversary. To be sure, many words are written on zoning problems, but these are mostly found in the opinions of appellate courts, or in rehash and reinterpretation of those opinions. The really good and thoughtful and valuable books on zoning can be counted on the fingers of one hand.

The trouble is—aside from the boredom of the younger players of the zoning game—that the stuff being written, including the great bulk of the opinions from the bench, is almost wholly "library research." Most zoning literature could be compared with the sort of passionate love stories that might be written by a cloistered celibate.

This book has been written by an enthusiastic participant in the zoning game, one who is neither cloistered nor celibate. In no sense is it library research. When Dick Babcock cites a case, it comes out as naturally as a biblical quotation rolls from the lips of the preacher. He has not spent a couple of frantic hours with *Corpus Juris Secundum* looking for something to prove his point.

Babcock has been an active player in the zoning game. After all, the zoning controversies that end in an appellate court (where he has appeared for both municipalities and property owners) represent only a small proportion of the cases that are heard by a lower court (where Babcock has also appeared) and these in turn are a very tiny fraction of the zoning actions that never go to court at all (and here too Babcock has represented and advised developers, private owners, and local governments). This sort of experience impels an author to be less than sweetly patient with the type of publication that has more footnotes than substance.

Finally, not content with resting his case on his personal experience only, Babcock traveled across the country and into Europe, interviewing planners, lawyers, developers, and judges. He wanted to see the zoning game as it *is* played, not as it *should be* played, according to the library researchers. This book is the result.

Perhaps because it is still so young, or perhaps because it is a rather violent disruption of man's pseudo-sacred rights in property, zoning is an institution that largely reflects the idea of certain strong men: Bassett, the father of zoning; Bettman, the brilliant apologist; Pomeroy, the flamboyant prophet. Babcock, the combatant, bids to be another of those whose name will be long remembered by players in the zoning game.

In this book he calls me an irrelevant poet. Dick Babcock is also a poet of sorts. Which means that he is to be allowed poetic license—which he has used. He also has a sense of humor, which may do much to relieve the ennui of those who are bored with zoning.

I agree with most of Babcock's remarks about planners (of which sect I am a member), but feel that he may have been too charitable toward the other groups. Perhaps the others agree with his remarks about themselves, but believe he has been soft on planners. In any case, I think, and hope, that Babcock's analysis will stir up at least a little storm among all of us.

I disagree with some of the points he makes. But then, if I read only those things with which I agree, it would be a dull world for me.

Nevertheless, this book has been fun to read. More than that, it makes a number of points that need to be made. And it definitely adds another volume to that brief list I spoke of earlier, the good and thoughtful and valuable books on zoning.

Dennis O'Harrow

Chicago
March, 1966

Contents

Introduction

> "And so put off the weary day
> When we would have to put our mind
> On how to crowd but still be kind."
> Robert Frost

THIS is foremost a statement of opinion, and only incidentally one of fact. This circumstance should be refreshing in the arena of the social sciences where collecting facts has achieved an unparalleled status. I feel entitled to this conceit, having demonstrated my skill at *that* game by spawning a law review article with 310 footnotes. The proclivity to data gathering is, of course, not limited to city planning. The tendency of the planners to shuffle and reshuffle facts may explain, nevertheless, why the oracular style of Lewis Mumford and the petulance of Jane Jacobs have attracted so much attention. The sheer volume of this data collecting reminds me of Justice Holmes's wail of anguish on receiving at his summer retreat one more crate of statistics on the garment industry from Justice Brandeis.

Hunch and gut reaction are apparent in these observations. These are appropriate benchmarks in a field where scrutiny of entrails for propitious omens frequently is more effective than the most careful search in the academic publications. There are, of course, various responsible ways to gather empirical data about a social or political process, and in many situations such effort is not only appropriate but imperative. Statistical analysis just does not happen to be meaningful in the fractured area of zoning. The methods of the anthropologist make more sense. In any event, this commentary is not that of a social statistician but of an advocate and observer in the field for twenty years who has had the unique opportunity, offered by the Ford Foundation in 1962, to tour this country and England interviewing lawyers, judges, city planners, and interested laymen. The tapes of these conversations are extensively relied on throughout this book.

Before dipping into the substance of these remarks, I want to set out their general boundaries.

These observations are generally limited to the field of municipal zoning.[1] In that joust I have acquired my scars, and it is in that area that we have the greatest experience of any of the fields embraced by land-use planning. I leave to others the detailed analysis of the malevolent influence that local tax structure has had upon our land development and redevelopment. If it is the American policy to give the individual freedom of choice, then there can be no doubt, as Arthur Gallion, former Dean of the School of Architecture at the University of Southern California has observed, that the present system of local taxation, which imposes a penalty on new buildings while it encourages competition from old buildings, is inimical to that policy. This book is also silent on that new art of land-use policy broadly identified as urban renewal. The air is so heavy with charges and countercharges concerning the social and political implications of this adolescent technique that he would be a foolish commentator who attempted to evaluate, with any hope of accuracy, the course of renewal at this time.

Zoning law, in contrast, has developed sufficiently in the last four decades to have some form to its flesh, but it is not yet so ancient that it is hopeless to undertake some surgery. Since the early days of zoning when attorney Edward Bassett attempted to make some sense out of zoning law, thousands of communities have been disposing of zoning disputes without any significant awareness that they were participating in a law-making process which might embrace a body of principles. If this is because there are no principles by which the execution of zoning law is capable of being measured, then it is time to acknowledge this dreary fact. If, however, there are such principles, then it is time to put them out where they can be subject to scrutiny, not in separate and isolated municipal forums but in a political arena where as large a consensus as possible may weigh their usefulness in a democratic society.

These observations will fall into two well-defined but not mutually exclusive categories: a commentary upon the words and deeds of the lay and professional participants, and a few suggestions on the appropriate bases for decision-making.

The participants in zoning are, on the professional side, the practicing attorneys, the judges, and the city planners. It is these professionals, whether in the law or planning, who, I have sensed during fifteen years in the pit of zoning and planning litigation, are either too bored, ignorant, or fearful to speak out effectively. These remarks are also directed to the lay decision-makers, both public and private. In the public sector they are the administrators or local legislators, particularly in our suburbs, who are confident that governmental corruption is only a matter of black bags and who are offended if anyone suggests that the use of such land-use tools as zoning can involve less obvious forms of civic dishonesty.[2] In the private sector the principal decision-maker is the developer or builder; the Ishmael of land development, if one believes the planners and local lay officials.

Examination of the motives and bias of each of these actors is, I believe, useful, not only because zoning's pretensions have not all been canonized but also because much of what does take place in this field is not discernable from the literature. Of all the areas of the law, zoning is the least susceptible to academic scrutiny. In no other field of the law is it so difficult to grub out what is taking place from the court decisions, professional journals, and model statutes. A vast amount of the decision-making is not on record. When it is available it is often devoted in such detail to the minute facts of individual cases that it is almost impossible to marshal, much less analyze, the bases of decisions.

In the second half of this book I propose a reexamination of the myths of zoning; to ask who put the hot pepper in Mr. Bassett's chowder.

Zoning, including its administration and its judicial review, represents the unique American contribution to the solution of disputes over competing demands for the use of private land. When there are conflicting interests, it is patently necessary for someone to determine which of these are valid in a society based upon the belief in private property and the mobility of the individual. First it is necessary to identify those interests. The question then arises who should and will referee the contest: the municipal legislature, the state legislature, the courts, or the administrators? Finally, it is appropriate to provide benchmarks by which the relative validity of the conflicting interests, public and private, should be measured.

In the second part an effort also will be made to examine the "principles" underlying zoning law, to urge the need for a reorientation of our attitudes toward the conflicts over land use and to suggest the direction that this restructuring should take.

A final preliminary note: the primary emphasis in this statement is upon suburban, not urban, activity. One hunts where the ducks are believed to be, and I do not have to labor the obvious change in the migratory patterns of the human pintail during the last two decades.

Richard F. Babcock
Member of the Illinois Bar

March, 1966

Part 1

The Players

I

The Stage – Historical and Current

Plus ça change, plus c'est la même chose

ZONING reached puberty in company with the Stutz Bearcat and the speakeasy. F. Scott Fitzgerald and the Lindy Hop were products of the same generation. Of all these phenomena of the twenties, only zoning has remained viable a generation later. If, in the beginning, zoning owed much to the fears of Fifth Avenue merchants in New York City that the garment industry would further encroach on their elegant sidewalks, zoning can thank the residents of the North Shores and Westchesters of this country for its remarkable survival. John Delafons, a recent English observer of American zoning, noted, "It was as a means of strengthening the institution of private property in the face of rapid and unsettling changes in the urban scene that zoning won such remarkable acceptance in American communities."[1]

To put it more specifically, zoning has provided the device for protecting the homogenous, single-family suburb from the city. University of Chicago Law School professor, Ernst Freund, saw this thirty years ago, when he stated, "Every one knows that the crux of the zoning problem lies in the residential district, and that when we speak of amenity we have in mind residential preference."[2]

The insulation of the single-family detached dwelling was the primary objective of the early zoning ordinances, and this objective is predominant today although in every other respect the zoning technique has undergone changes so dramatic as to make almost

3

impossible a comparison of the device as it appeared in the 1920's with its progeny four decades later. At the start, the concept of zoning was the result of some ingenious legal persuasion by sophisticated and knowledgeable lawyers who believed the courts could be induced to permit municipalities, by an extension of the common law nuisance doctrine, to build a comprehensive land-use regulatory scheme under the aegis of the police power. The United States Supreme Court in 1926 upheld zoning in the landmark case of *Village of Euclid v. Ambler Realty Co.*[3] because that conservative bench regarded the intrusion of industry *and apartments* into single-family zones as cousin to a public nuisance, similar to the intrusion of a tuberculosis sanitarium which could be kept out under orthodox common law principles. The Court stated, "A nuisance may be merely a right thing in the wrong place, like a pig in the parlor instead of the barnyard," and, after describing the noxious consequences of allowing an apartment house in a single-family zone, it concluded, "Under these circumstances, apartment houses, which in a different environment would be not only entirely unobjectionable but highly desirable, come very near to being nuisances."

Zoning was no more than a rational and comprehensive extension of public nuisance law, with the great advantage (over the common law nuisance) of providing all landowners with knowledge before the fact of what they could and could not do with their land. Alfred Bettman, the persuasive advocate, acknowledged this debt in his brief in support of zoning in the *Euclid* case:

> [T]he term [public nuisance] has ceased to have any definite meaning as a measure of legislative power. . . . A lawyer would often hardly hazard a guess as to whether his client's proposed industry will or will not be declared a nuisance. . . . The zone plan, by comprehensively districting the whole territory of the city and giving ample space and appropriate territory for each type of use, is decidedly more just, intelligent, and reasonable than the system, if system it can be called, of spotty ordinances and uncertain litigations about the definition of a nuisance.[4]

Once the legal hurdles were taken, zoning caught on not because of the sophistication of its early advocates but because it was simple in application. The typical ordinance of the 1920's divided the municipality into three zones—Single-Family, Commercial, and Industrial. If the community was sufficiently urbanized, an apartment district might be included, although the first New York City ordinance in 1916 did not distinguish in its districts between single-family homes and apartments, apparently because the drafters doubted the validity of a classification between single-family and multiple-family uses. (A more notable example of the clouded crystal ball is hard to imagine!) It was a simple matter to draw lines on the municipal street map showing the boundaries of the districts: six pages took care of the simple requirements for permitted uses, yards, and maximum height. There might be hardships in a local ordinance drawn in such broad strokes. To cope with particular instances of unfairness, the state legislation which empowered municipalities to zone provided that a local municipal board should have the power to grant "variances" from the requirements in cases of "hardship."

Drawn as it was to such an elementary scale, it was no wonder that this ingenious device swept the country in the twenties. It was apparent that one community could cut and paste into its local code another municipality's zoning ordinance. We latter-day critics regard early zoning as quite a fad. Professor Jesse Dukeminier, Jr., describes the early days:

> What often happened when zoning first swept the country was this: The city fathers called in an outside expert who made a swift survey of the city and then prepared a zoning map. If any master plan or surveys of physical, economic, and sociological conditions in the city were prepared, as likely as not they were filed away in a bottom drawer. The zoning map 'stabilized property values' and that was what the city fathers were interested in.[5]

Fred Bair, articulate curmudgeon and planning consultant who operates out of Auburndale, Florida, suggests that we have learned little in forty years:

Before this new device could be tested by experience, it was widely 'sold' around the country, much in the manner of present-day urban renewal. Progress on the municipal scene was measured in terms of how many additional cities had zoning each year, rather than by what was actually happening to cities.[6]

The primary, if not the exclusive, purpose in the 1920's was to protect the single-family district and that objective is foremost four decades later. Nothing else about this technique is recognizable after four decades of experimentation. Only if we remember that the central goal—the insulation of the single-family district—is unchanged, can we admire the vast changes in the devices which have been employed to further this immutable objective. Remarkable changes have occurred in the techniques of zoning because the simple tools of the early days, such as the elementary districting concept, sufficient in an era when home building and commercial development were principally the function of small, isolated, do-it-yourself entrepreneurs, are no longer adequate to do the job in the sixties. The massive outward thrust from the central urban area demands a far more sophisticated response on the part of the suburbs.

THE GROWTH OF "FLEXIBILITY"

The elementary concept of districting (each pig in its own pen) could not provide the agility a welterweight must have to defeat or at least to discourage a Goliath. Unable or, more accurately, unwilling, to join together to battle the metropolitan explosion and the sophisticated developmental techniques of the land promoters, the suburbs have seized upon each new device conceived by the planners to parry the blows of these formidable antagonists. Nowhere is this ingenuity more apparent than in the administrative devices which have been invented to provide the suburban communities with the discretion necessary to meet each new proposal of those who would challenge their security.

The earliest device was the so-called variance to be granted by the board of appeals or board of adjustment. The 1923 Standard

State Zoning Enabling Act, published by the United States Department of Commerce and widely adopted, described the variance device as follows:

> The board of adjustment shall have the following powers:
>
> .   .   .   .
>
> 3. To authorize upon appeal in specific cases such variance from the terms of the ordinance as will not be contrary to the public interest, where, owing to special conditions, a literal enforcement of the provisions of the ordinance will result in unnecessary hardship, and so that the spirit of the ordinance shall be observed and substantial justice done.

Although the variance remains in most of our zoning ordinances, its crude use to grant and deny favors was subjected to substantial criticism, not only from the courts but from the professional writers as well. The indictment has been that, far from being a safety valve, the variance is a handy gimmick to permit "leakage" from the certainty provided by the concept of districting. Today the variance has become a rather small bore weapon in the arsenal of the municipality, not because of the criticism directed against it but because of its inadequacy as a device for meeting the pressures placed upon our municipalities by the developers and by the outsiders who wish to come into the municipality.

Shortly after World War II a more effective technique for making use of the *ad hoc,* discretionary decision became popular; namely, the so-called special permit (also known as the special use, conditional use, or special exception). In the text of the ordinance for each district there were listed a few uses which would be permitted not as a matter of right but at the discretion of the local authority. By this method the post-war community could look over each proposal which, in its judgment, might raise a problem. Appropriate as a device to control the location of the facilities of public utilities that did not fit into the trilogy of residential, commercial, and industrial uses, the special permit was seized upon as a method for postponing zoning decisions on unpopular activities of the type recently catalogued by the New Jersey Supreme

Court as "trailer camps, motels, slaughterhouses, glue works and the like."[7]

It was the enthusiastic and unprincipled use of the special permit device that led Detroit planner-lawyer Walter Blucher to exclaim: "The question must be asked seriously whether zoning, as it is currently being practiced, is endangering our democratic institutions. . . . Is zoning increasingly becoming the rule of man rather than the rule of law? I would be inclined to answer both questions affirmatively."[8] The municipalities could not care less about the protests of the professionals.

The special permit, however, was not sufficiently flexible to provide municipalities with the resilience which was absolutely essential during the era after World War II in order to deal with the Levittowns and similar developments of a scale too large ever to be controlled by special permits. The municipalities were not, however, at a loss. There appeared a more sophisticated concept the floating zone, a technique where a particular category of uses was identified in the text of the ordinance but no equivalent area was found on the map. Given the "right" proposal put forward by the "right" developer, this textual reference would descend from the firmament and settle on the lucky owner's land—but only after extensive and careful bargaining between the applicant and municipal legislature. In one of the first cases to test the device that was later to be tagged the "floating zone," *Rodgers v. Village of Tarrytown,*[9] the highest appellate court in New York described the ordinance this way:

> The 1947 ordinance creates 'A new district or class of zone . . . [to] be called "Residence B-B," ' in which, besides one- and two-family dwellings, buildings for multiple occupancy of fifteen or fewer families were permitted. The boundaries of the new type district were not delineated in the ordinance but were to be 'fixed by amendment of the official village building zone map, at such times in the future as such district or class of zone is applied, to properties in this village.'

The court rejected the contention that the ordinance was invalid because it set no boundaries for the new district and made no changes in the zoning map:

> It may be conceded that, under the method which the board did adopt, no one will know, from the 1947 ordinance itself, precisely where a Residence B-B district will ultimately be located. But since such a district is simply a garden apartment development, we find nothing unusual or improper in that circumstance. The same uncertainty—as to the location of the various types of structures—would be present if a zoning ordinance were to sanction garden apartments as well as one-family homes in a Residence A district—and yet there would be no doubt as to the propriety of that procedure.

Judge Albert Conway, who dissented, viewed this innovation differently:

> The decision here made gives judicial sanction to a novel and unprecedented device whereby the board of trustees of a village may, in the exercise of its discretion, authorize the erection of multiple family dwellings on property, located wholly within established districts theretofore uniformly zoned for use as one- or two-family dwellings, by the simple expedient of declaring, upon the application of individuals owning a certain acreage, that henceforth such property shall constitute a new and separate zoning district. The device may have much to commend it in the way of administrative convenience, but it most assuredly is not 'zoning,' as that term has previously been understood.

> .   .   .   .

> [A] person purchasing property in Tarrytown in a Residence A or B district to bring up his children now has no way of knowing whether the property next to his may or may not become the site of a multiple family dwelling with the attendant increases in population, traffic dangers, commerce and congestion.

Most recently, there has been brought before the courts the most ingenious technique of all: "contract zoning." Unlike the variance, the special permit, or the floating zone, contract zoning does not require that the municipality preannounce in its ordinance any of its intentions, however equivocal. Everything appears regular and uniform on the face of the ordinance, in both the map and in the text. The mandate from the state enabling act to divide the community into districts and to specify in advance the rules of the game is not flaunted by provisions such as the special permit or the floating zone which admit on the face of the ordinance that certainty is not available in the local law. Under contract zoning, certainty is assured in every paragraph of the text, in every section of the map. It is only when the developer seeks a change from, say, Residential to Commercial that he discovers that conditions will be attached by way of covenant or contract which do not appear in the text of the Commercial District. When he achieves his rezoning he has not obtained what the text promises him but only what the particular legislature sitting at that time is willing to give him. The late Andrew Dallstream, a distinguished Chicago lawyer and former Chairman of the Cook County Board of Zoning Appeals, once described one method for using the device:

> When the Board [of Zoning Appeals] has before it a request for a changed, but non-objectionable, use, it will often submit, after hearing, a report recommending the change to the County Commissioners. In its findings the Board will recite that the owner-applicant has volunteered to alienate his property to a third party and to reacquire it subject to a covenant running with the land specifically prohibiting objectionable uses. The covenants conventionally recite that their terms inure to the benefit of and may be enforced by inhabitants of the county—in some cases, property owners within a specified radius—in which the premises are located.[10]

The property is rezoned Commercial and on the face of the ordinance a dozen or score of uses are permitted. But in fact, by means of a private covenant required by a public body only one or two uses are authorized.

I know of no more candid evaluation of the objectives of this recent ploy than that given me by the beloved Hugh Pomeroy, planner sans parallel, and for many years prior to his death in 1961 the Planning Director of Westchester County, New York. He was speaking of the problem encountered in a municipality in Westchester County where the community (and Hugh) wanted to permit a heavy commercial use to come into what was then a rather light retail district. Hugh said to me: "I don't think it should be handled on a special permit basis because if the special permit method is properly used you establish standards that would make it possible to do this elsewhere in the classification. I've come to the conclusion, and the village attorney with me, both of us a little disturbed by it, that the thing to do is to reclassify subject to limitations."[11]

In other words, the municipality will not, unless compelled, provide a rule of law which will be applicable in similar situations. That this condition should exist today can be explained only by the inability of the old techniques to forestall adequately those symptoms of urban growth which are distasteful to the suburban dweller.

The latest and unquestionably the most complex of the flexibility techniques is the Planned Unit Development. This is "contract zoning" with sophistication and—where fairly administered—a substantially greater degree of candor. The municipality inserts a section in the text of its ordinance authorizing the development of land without regard to the customary lot size requirements, or the segregation of housing types or, indeed, of uses, provided the specific plan of development meets with the approval of the local authorities. Customarily the ordinance requires the assembly of substantial acreage and the submission for approval of a plan showing densities, types of dwellings, use, location, and management of common open space, and the location and nature of nonresidential facilities. Each proposal is judged on its particular merits, and the standards by which a proposal will be judged are vague. In effect, the Planned Unit Development device supplants the preexisting zoning. Covenants and easements bargained for between developer and municipality take the place of customary zoning regulations. Preregulation gives way to negotiation.

THE CHAOS

That this metamorphosis in zoning from the simple, open-faced text to highly complex documents has resulted in total confusion does not need to be debated. Nor should it be pretended that there is not a valid place in the American litany for disorder. Anyone who attacks chaos as a way of life must answer to the American social tradition reflected in our antitrust laws and in our devotion— at least our spoken devotion—to nongovernment: that the less the pre-regulation whether in the marketplace or in the social order, the more vigorous the society. But the chaos in land-use planning is not the result of uncontrolled individual enterprise. It is a result of a combination of controls and lack of controls, of over-planning and anti-planning, enterprise and anti-enterprise, all in absolute disarray. I doubt that even the most intransigent disciple of anarchy ever wished for or intended the litter that prevails in the area of local land-use regulation.

Mr. Bair again: "What is said here is not a plea for the status quo. Zoning will not stand still, and considering the shape it is in, nobody in his right mind should want it to. But the change should be in the direction of improvement, rather than a move from occasional mild disorder to universal chaos."[12] This is not a latter-day attack. In 1931 William Munro, then Vice President of the National Municipal League, protested that the original purpose of zoning had become distorted:

> Zoning, however, quickly became popular. . . .
> The rank and file of the people are coming to look upon [zoning] as merely a matter of maintaining or increasing property values. Whenever a question of rezoning comes up, the issue is not usually approached from the standpoint of what the city needs, but of what the private owners desire and what their immediate neighbors feel disinclined to let them have.[13]

This disordered condition is attributable to a number of circumstances, not all of which are unique to this field of the law.

First, we have the multiplicity of jurisdictions, the innumerable decision-makers. In other significant areas of administrative law— the regulation of utilities, control over the issuance of securities, and the arbitration of disputes between employer and employee— there exist if not national at least statewide forums for the resolution of disputes. In the area of zoning there is no such centralized umpire to provide a sense of belonging to a common administrative practice, and, indeed, of sharing a common administrative ethic. Among these scattered groups of lay decision-makers there is an almost total lack of communication despite the efforts of innumerable planning groups, each offering earnest if generally diffused guidance. One of the most significant results of this fractured decision-making process is that the injunctions of the judiciary have only nominal impact upon the decision-makers. If the Supreme Court of California makes a determination that the California Public Utilities Commission has acted improperly, the impact of that judicial determination is direct and, in most instances, decisive. But if the Supreme Court of California were to say to the local legislature in Community X that its policy is improper that injunction, I suspect, would have little practical impact upon the identical administrative actions of Community Y or perhaps even on Community X itself. Other lawyers have shared the experience that follows a victory on behalf of a landowner in the state Supreme Court. You have obtained a decision that the single-family classification of your client's property is unreasonable. Your client wants to use the property for commercial purposes. The community immediately rezones the property to a Duplex Zone and invites you to spend another two years and thousands of dollars litigating *that* classification.

This indifference to judicial decisions applies, by the way, even in jurisdictions such as Maryland, where, as in Baltimore County, there are relatively few independent municipalities and decisions with respect to land use are centralized in the county itself. One Maryland attorney put it to me this way:

> And the trouble is, of course, that when we are dealing with lay boards of appeals, as we are probably in most of the jurisdictions, they aren't even aware of the decisions of the Maryland Court of Appeals. And from a practical point of view, the Maryland Court of Appeals can write all the opinions it wants to, and they aren't really sure, exactly, what the Court of Appeals intended in the case.

If the Court of Appeals in the case which I spoke to you about re-
manded to the board of appeals for further hearing, I don't think
these people would be competent to know exactly what the Court of
Appeals meant.

The converse is also true. Court decisions for or against a city's
ordinance are popularly thought of as some magic amulet or hex
which affect the validity of other applications of the same zoning
ordinance in completely unrelated cases. For example, a client
once consulted me wishing to build a duplex in a single-family
zone in Wilmette, Illinois. I advised him his case was somewhat
tenuous. A few weeks later the Illinois Supreme Court decided in
favor of a gasoline company that had sought to build in a restricted
retail zone on the other side of the same village. Discovering this,
the client called again, assuming that this new decision so weakened
the fiber of the ordinance that it was ripe for the kill. He found
it hard to understand that some older cases involving duplexes
in more distant places like Mt. Prospect and Chicago might have
more relevance to his problem than a brand new gas station case
from the same town.

The extent of the chaos is also attributable to the variety of
judicial attitudes toward the content of "general welfare" in the
zoning field. The protest of the property-oriented lawyer in California or New Jersey that the courts of his state give unlimited
scope to municipal restrictions on private development must sound
like a voice from Mars to the frustrated municipal attorney in
Minnesota or Ohio, who must defend his client's puniest regulatory efforts under the jaundiced eye of his state's appellate courts.

It is this vast gulf among judicial attitudes in the states toward
the police power that makes zoning law—even more than other
areas of the law relating to real estate—so variegated. In zoning
procedure, the lack of uniformity from state to state is perhaps
understandable in terms of the established localism of things relating to real estate. It is apparent with all aspects of the law of
private real property, mortgages, title, and conveyance, that rules
are bound to be diverse and peculiarly local in character. But in

none of these other related controls over real property is there the wide spectrum for judicial improvisation that is provided in zoning by the policy issues circling around the police power and substantive due process, and by the sweeping generalizations of state enabling legislation.

Zoning law is public law in a sense that neither mortgages nor title are, and it is doubtful whether the analogy to other phases of real property is conclusive. The treatment of zoning law as a branch of local real estate law rather than as a branch of constitutional law, and the resulting differences between states, is largely due to the unwillingness of the United States Supreme Court to see zoning as regulations affecting people and not just as regulations affecting land. The justices are accustomed to dealing with the blatant forms of discrimination found in the school segregation and legislative gerrymandering cases, and do not recognize the importance of the more subtle forms of discrimination found in the zoning area. Consequently, the United States Supreme Court has let each state go its own way in creating its own rules.

A further explanation for the disheveled condition of the law of land-use control lies in the varying social attitudes toward zoning. These depend upon the stage of urbanization in the particular locality—a point which I intend to develop later. To the extent that these local attitudes are reflected in the law, the rules are bound to look like Joseph's coat.

Finally, the persistence of the chaos owes a good deal to the failure of anyone to come up with an alternative which a court or legislature could accept if it decided to stamp out some of the current abuses.

The paradox of zoning is that in the face of this anarchy there has developed a pantheon of myths, a condition remarkable in so adolescent an art. Yet the myths, while operating to block intelligent reappraisal of our practices, have not offered the saving grace of cohesiveness, which would provide, if nothing else, a sense of security. Because we no longer invoke the social hazards of highway robbery and furtive fornication to justify the regulation of billboards, do not suppose we have achieved a plateau of rational analysis. Florida planning consultant Fred Bair has done more than his share in ticking off the myths, if not in demolishing them. Why do zoning ordinances require a yard? Why is a multiple-family dwelling, as one court pontificated, "not inherently benign?" Why are there density controls over apartments nestled in the jungle of commercial buildings in the central city? Why must there be 600 square feet of floor space in a house to be reasonably "healthy, safe and moral?" Let Fred explain:

> You go up and talk to the American Public Health Association and say:
> "Look—we've been reading this housing code of yours with considerable interest. Where did you come up with the figure that you had to have 600 square feet of floor space in a house to be reasonably healthy, safe and moral—or whatever it is that you're trying to do with that regulation?" And they say, "Well—what was that again?" And you say, "Well, where did you get that 600 square foot figure?" "Well, gee, let's see—who was on that committee?" So you find out that Stu Chapin and so-and-so and so-and-so were on that committee in 1952 and they reached up and picked a figure out of thin air. This conclusion is inescapable. But because the figure was published by APHA, it became a religious symbol. And now you go into them and say, "Well, look—we've got air conditioning. We've got heating. We've got artificial light. Got any number of things that we didn't have generally in 1940 or 1950 or whatever. Does this change the picture?" And they say, "Well, no—it doesn't change the picture. It is printed right there—600 square feet." And you can pursue our symbols and shibboleths back to their origins and find out how flimsy are the origins. But because these things are universally worshipped now, the fact that the origins were a little weak doesn't make too much difference any longer.

I used to feel sad that so youthful a technique would so early establish a formidable stable of dogma. My reaction has now changed to one of perplexed admiration that the confusion which characterizes zoning thrives in the same culture in which the myth flourishes so abundantly.

WHO CARES?

Are we wasting our time on a matter of interest only to a small group of professionals? Is this compartment of the law significant?

No one is enthusiastic about zoning except the people. The non-people—the professionals—hope it gets lost. The judges find zoning a monumental bore, most lawyers consider it a nuisance, and the planners treat it as a cretinous member of the planning family about whom the less said the better. Yet thousands of local officials regard zoning as the greatest municipal achievement since the perfection of public sanitary systems. Zoning is the urban renewal (or more accurately the urban reversal) of the village, the answer to the suburban maiden's prayer. I become tired of the planner's cry that zoning is a failure. By the test of acceptance in the market place, zoning has been a smashing success. To the dweller on the urban fringe the usefulness of zoning as an exclusionary technique both present and potential must seem unlimited. If you doubt it, I invite you to examine the consequences of such respectable techniques as large-acre zoning and minimum house size regulations.

Quantitative evidence during the last decade of the remarkable change in significance of zoning is equally impressive. One need look no further than the treatment of the subject in our law digests, the remarkable change in the agendas of conventions of state municipal associations, the contents of law reviews and the dockets of our intermediate and top appellate courts. The grant in 1963 of half a million dollars by the Ford Foundation to the American Law Institute to undertake a major reappraisal of land-use law is evidence of the most practical sort that land-use policies are no longer of only parochial interest. The new horizons of concern with this field are evident in the growing interest of mortgage lenders and title guaranty companies. One very large national insurance company has concluded that is must have a legal opinion on zoning before it makes any major commercial loan. The President of Home Title Guaranty Company, New York, has said, in a study of zoning published by his company:

Even though zoning violations can render a title unmarketable, it is not possible today to write an insurance policy covering such violations with any reasonable degree of assurance. This is because present-day zoning laws, regulations and practice are too variable and unpredictable. We do not expect at this time to write a zoning insurance policy, but, at Home Title Guaranty Company, we still feel a responsibility to study zoning and make the benefit of such study available to our attorney customers.

· · · · · · · · · · · ·

We have published this monograph as a service to lawyers and their clients and in an effort to help clear up some of the misunderstandings about zoning. We also hope that we are pointing the way toward laws and regulations covering zoning so codified and clear that the subject can be handled with confidence.[14]

If this corner of our law is significant as well as chaotic it merits more thoughtful examination than it has received. This job is being undertaken in orthodox academic fashion by those more qualified than I, and I prefer to talk in more subjective prose. It is time someone spoke of land-use regulation in terms of those who make or influence the decisions rather than as though these decisions were arrived at in some antiseptic chamber without the aid of human impulse. I have searched for papers in the arena of land-use planning on what makes tick a planner, a judge, a lawyer, a plan commission member, a legislator, a developer, to find instead articles on the role of the plan commission member, or the goals of the community. Inspirational themes, indeed, but hardly adequate when one is evaluating a current social phenomenon. Thus this venture into the subjective: a suggestion of what prompts the layman, the planner, the judge, and the lawyer to act as they do in the charged area of control over private land use.

II

The Layman as Public Decision-Maker

"The law cannot disregard the real importance of the
illogical in human affairs."

Dissent, *Goldman* v. *Crowther,*
147 Md 282, 285

EVERY time I pick up one of the early books on zoning
such as Edward Bassett's *Zoning,* and check a few pages, I
have the warm glow that comes with reading a romantic account
of some municipal Graustark where a bunch of happy, well-informed people with a social I.Q. of 150 sit around making decisions in complete freedom from outside pressure and without the
slightest concern for what takes place anywhere but in their duchy.

My experience during the past two decades indicates that these
people are still making zoning decisions without the slightest concern for the outside world. Whether they are happy, well-informed,
and socially attuned is another matter. Certainly they operate in
the belief that their balkanized municipal universe is the happiest
of worlds.

Local control over use of private land has withstood with incredible resilience the centripetal political forces of the last generation. In an era of concentration of power, each blind man may
offer a different explanation for the remarkable continuing strength
of local control over land use. I believe this condition is explained
in part by the conviction of the local decision-maker that he is
more competent to decide these questions than is his professional
counterpart in Albany, Columbus, or Sacramento. The layman

19

remains king in land-use matters because he has not feared to grasp the nettle of land-use regulation. In matters cosmic like unemployment and the disposal of metropolitan sanitary and industrial waste, the layman as public decision-maker has a sense of inadequacy or boredom. Not so, however, on the question of who or what comes in on the lot next door. I have often wanted to test this theory in a restaurant. Imagine the wholesale indifference were you to poll the luncheon guests on their attitude toward a proposed bill to reform the state criminal laws or the banking code. You might, with luck, strike a penologist or a banker, but the rest of the guests would regard you as some sort of eccentric. Try the same test, however, with a proposal to revise drastically our laws on the control over use of private land and half of the guests would come off their seats. Not only does this public law have a greater direct impact upon the layman's social and economic security, but he is certain that he knows what is good for him as well as any professional.

The intriguing fact about the citizen as decision-maker in this area of such dominant social overtones is that the hoary political labels of "conservative" and "liberal" are meaningless when we talk about zoning.

THE CONSERVATIVE AND ZONING

We can reasonably assume that most residents of rural and suburban areas in all parts of this country are generally political and economic conservatives. This is evident in attitudes toward federal spending, labor, and candidates for national political office. When it comes to zoning, however, one of these same people will regard it as an outrageous intrusion upon individual freedom, while two others will see it as the greatest thing to come down the road since the Coolidge inauguration. I offer you four illustrations: Winnetka, Illinois; Parsipanny, New Jersey; Ogle County, Illinois; and Houston, Texas, hardly suburban, but a frontier nonetheless.

Winnetka, Illinois is a leafy, lakeside suburb north of Chicago where the median income per family is around $20,000, the vote is better than 2 to 1 Republican, and a well-deserved reputation for civic virtue is relished without much reflection on the insignificance of the municipal temptations that goodness must resist. Although there are rare aberrations, it is fair to say that the inhabitant of Winnetka is conservative in every sense of the word—and that he regards the zoning ordinance as an essential weapon in his battle with the forces of darkness. He is right. Zoning and its companion, the subdivision ordinance, have been major factors in preserving the character of the community: the integrity, if you will, of the large lot, detached single-family residence. If Winnetka is troubled today by pressures for varied dwelling types it is reassured by the knowledge that most of its land area is built upon; and it can feel that it is dealing with the problem by debating the risks of providing multiple-family dwellings for elderly Presbyterians. Zoning in Winnetka is respectable. Anyone that challenges it is, if not a money-grubbing parvenu, obviously a wild-eyed dreamer intent upon foisting his ideas of social mobility upon the few remaining enclaves of gracious living.

In these attitudes the resident of Winnetka is, of course, no different from his neighbors along Chicago's North Shore or New York's Westchester County, or indeed in the exurbs of New Jersey.

Take, for example, the New Jersey Township of Parsipanny, where a belief in free enterprise reigns supreme—as long as the enterprise is exercised somewhere else. Witness the experience of the developer who wanted to carry on the tradition of the American Frontier and make a profit by filling in a swamp and subdividing the land. Unfortunately for him, however, the local powers wanted his swamp for a wildlife preserve. Condemn the land? How crude! How much easier to zone it into "The Indeterminate Zone Classification" where, as a practical matter, the only possible use was a hunt club or a preserve. The local burghers no doubt did this without losing any sleep, convinced that they were protecting the sanctity of their Elysian fields from corruption. How many of them really comprehended when Justice Hall of the state supreme court told them they had violated the plaintiff's property rights? "There cannot be the slightest doubt from the evidence," the court said, "the the prime object of the zone regulations is to retain the land substantially in its natural state."[1]

The use of zoning to keep land vacant is a very real if rarely declared objective of the resident of suburbia. I still relish the indiscreet comment of one objector who was testifying in opposition to a proposal to rezone from single-family to multiple-family a parcel which abutted a commercial district in Highland Park, Illinois. "I would," he blurted, "rather have the lots in their present natural wooded beauty." This, to him, was a perfectly proper function of zoning.

Perhaps the most fascinating aspect of the suburb's attitude toward zoning is its conviction that any weapon is legitimate as long at it does not involve the type of financial venality the suburbanite attributes to the decision-makers in the large city. In a lawsuit involving a Chicago suburb, the entire right-of-way of a suburban railroad was zoned for single-family residence purposes whether the line was passing through a residential area or was bounded on both sides by commercial development. Prior to the lawsuit the railroad sought to have an unused portion of the right-of-way in a commercial area reclassified to commercial so that an existing gas station could be enlarged. (There happened to be three other gas stations on the three other corners of the intersection.) The village, understandably anticipating that this would result in requests from the railroad to rezone other parts of the right-of-way in the commercial area, asked for a delay of six months so that its planning consultant could prepare a report on the problem of what to do with the entire right-of-way. To this the railroad agreed, provided it could have a copy of the completed report. About five months later the attorney for the railroad returned to his office from a morning in court to find a manila envelope from the village hall on his desk. He was greeted by his secretary, who reported that she had received two phone calls from the village manager's office advising that the attorney had been sent the "wrong" report!

The "wrong report" was entitled "A Supplementary Report Upon Recommended Village Policy For Use of Rights-of-Way."

The document contained no reference to any other report. It was sympathetic to the railroad's position: if the municipality desired to keep land in the business areas as open space the reasonable approach for the village was to buy or condemn the property.

The attorney for the railroad photostated the report and returned the original to the village hall. The next day he received another report entitled "Report Upon Recommended Village Policy for Use of Rights-of-Way." This report, however, was sympathetic to the village's desire to maintain the residential zoning without compensation and full of court citations and legal arguments (this from a planner) why this course was valid! Later the attorney was advised that these two "separate" reports had originally been delivered to the village as one integrated document but upon request of an agent of the village had been returned to the planning consultant to be placed under separate covers. Through an egregious mistake the railroad's lawyer had been sent the "wrong" report.

Apparently, to the agent's sense of values there was absolutely nothing wrong in this way of dealing. Indeed, there was a definite belief that anyone who presumed to challenge this practice was guilty of lese majesty. It is this type of frequently encountered attitude that has led many attorneys to feel more sure of the fairness in the forum of the big city than in that of the suburb.

The secure resident of a community like Winnetka or Parsipanny has his equally conservative counterpart in Ogle County, a rich and beautiful agricultural area about 70 miles west of Chicago, where feeder cattle outnumber humans, and Democrats outnumber whooping cranes, but barely. About four years ago I was hired in conjunction with planning consultant Robert Piper, now with the American Institute of Architects in Washington, to prepare a zoning ordinance for this pristine county. We drafted an ordinance of a rather moderate cast but the farmers mounted an angry campaign against it in which the effective charge was that zoning was an unconstitutional and socialistic attempt to tell a man what he could do with his private property. Zoning was, in the words of the fero-

Citizens of Ogle County!

How would ZONING *"Private Property Control" affect you?*

Are you willing to give up private property rights you now enjoy?

Do you want your children *prevented from using their property in the ways you have used yours?*

Investigate ZONING *"Private Property Control" proposals now . . . before it's too late.* There will be no referendum. *See the maps at the County Clerk's office.*

Ask your supervisor to show you the regulations *which would affect your zone . . . or ask a member of the undersigned committee.*

Support the Committee to Oppose ZONING *"Private Property Control" in Ogle county. Send contributions to Raymond Buker, treasurer, 308 S. 8th st., Oregon. Ill.*

THE FOLLOWING ARE SOME OF THE MEMBERS OF THE COMMITTEE:
Keith S. Wood, chairman, 704 Jackson st., Oregon, phone 2–6189
James L. Cartwright, secretary, route 2, Oregon, phone 2–7143
Raymond Buker, treasurer, 308 S. 8th st., Oregon, phone 2–2206
David H. Martin, route 3, Oregon, phone 2–2258
O. C. Nelson, route 3, Oregon, phone 2–7308
Harriet Lowden Madlener, Sinnissippi farm, Oregon, phone 2–2433
Mr. and Mrs. R. B. McLaughlin, Rock River farms, Byron

Advertisement from the Ogle County, Illinois, *Rochelle News,* August 30, 1961 cious newspaper advertisements, a radical, un-American New Deal-ish device.

"The peasants of Europe came to America and became free men. If we allow this zoning law to pass we will be on the road back to peasantry in Ogle County."[2] So ran the ads in Ogle County. Imagine telling the Winnetkan that his favorite municipal tool had turned him into a peasant. Indeed! Yet residents of Winnetka and Ogle County are predominantly conservative, and share the same convictions about a score of economic and social issues. The paradox is more apparent than real. America's number one value is financial success. In Winnetka the ground rules call for doing money-making only in Chicago; local money-making is bad. In Ogle County the ultimate goal is no different but there is as yet no such substantial distinction between home and the market place.

Lest you assume that Ogle County represented nothing more than rural reaction, consider Houston, Texas, the only city over 100,000 population in the United States without a zoning ordinance.

Houston is the hair shirt of the city planners. When the talk gets dolorous at planning conventions and the planners' accumulated frustrations over zoning spill out on the bar, some poor soul is bound to suggest that zoning must stink because Los Angeles has had zoning for forty years, Houston never, and what the hell is the the difference! There is a difference and, while my point here does not permit the telling of the full and delectable tale of Houston, I have digressed so frequently that one more side path should not strain your patience much more.

Land-use control in Houston has for generations depended upon the private restrictive covenant placed in the deeds and plats by the developer. Almost every acre of land in the city is subjected to private restrictions over use, size, or cost of house, yard requirements, height of building, and all the other baggage customarily found in our zoning ordinances. Houston has considered the wisdom of adopting a zoning ordinance on more than one occasion. Shortly after World War II the matter was put to an unofficial referendum by an insecure city administration and was clobbered. This dispute, incidentally, became a private contest between those two distinguished citizens of Houston, Jesse Jones, an enthusiastic supporter of zoning, and Roy Cullen, who bitterly opposed it. Since both men enjoyed considerable public attention and Mr. Jones owned a newspaper there could be no complaint that the issue was ignored. Indeed, in a remarkable display of objectivity, *The Chronicle,* owned by Jones, made the front page of its issue of January 29, 1948, available to Mr. Cullen for an expression of opinion in opposition to the proposed zoning.

The letter read as follows:

January 28, 1948

Gov. Wm. P. Hobby
The Houston Post

Mr. George Cottingham
The Houston Chronicle

Mr. George Carmack
The Houston Press

Dear Sirs:

I believe the people of Houston should hear both sides of any question that might affect their lives. I sent you a statement about zoning that I asked you to publish, and since you refused, I am making a statement to you now that you might publish.

It has been a great pleasure to me and my wife to help build a Houston Symphony to one of the best in the country; to help the Art Museum, which I did as director, endorsing their notes until they were paid; to help build the University of Houston and the Medical Center; but I cannot go along any further for I can see only graft and greed that will control our city from here out, so I am sending in my resignation as chairman of the board of regents of the University of Houston, as a member of the Medical Center, and every other organization of which I am a member.

It has been a pleasure to help build this city up to now, but Jesse Jones has been away from here most of the time for the last 25 or 30 years, and has come back to Houston and decided, with the influence of the press here, and the assistance of a bunch of New York Jews, to run our city, so I am going to give our city to Jesse and his crowd.

Yours very truly,
H. R. Cullen

Rumor has it that Mr. Cullen had been an early supporter of
zoning because he understood it would permit the immediate re-
moval of the slaughterhouse across the street from one of the buildings he had given to the University of Houston. When he was
advised that this silly technique was not capable of accomplishing
anything so purposeful, he turned against it. If so, Cullen reacted
exactly as did Professor Rexford Tugwell, hardly a political soul-
mate, but also an early supporter of zoning, who some years
previously had indicted zoning as an ineffectual, negative, and obsolescent tool of city planning.[3]

Houston tried again in 1962. Again an unofficial referendum, and
again it was buried, approximately 75,000 votes against, 50,000
for. For our purposes, the significant part of the tale rests with the
nature of the antagonists. By and large, the residents of the wealthy
subdivisions of River Oaks and Memorial Drive were indifferent.
They were sufficiently cohesive and wealthy to maintain a rigorous
legal patrol over their private covenants. If zoning was not needed
to protect the single-family area, there was no interest in the fight.
At the other end of the economic scale, the poor, pre-World War
II subdivisions—largely Negro—voted against zoning. After the
1962 vote the Mayor of Houston observed that his biggest disap-
pointment was that "those whom we expected to support us did
not." I would guess that this negative reaction was because in these
poorer neighborhoods substantially all the value had disappeared
from a residence as a home. The restrictive covenants had long
since been destroyed by indifference. All that remained was the
possibility of an increment of value from some ancillary commercial
use of the home: T. V. repair in the garage, a mom-and-dad grocery store in the front half of the house, storage in the yard, or conversions, all of which the proposed zoning ordinance purported
to forbid in residential districts. The articulate leaders of the anti-
zoners were primarily composed of substantial property owners and
real estate interests. They formed, of course, the "Greater Houston
Planning Association." Their ads proclaimed that zoning was radical and un-American. They told the Negro that zoning caused

slums, and their cartoons suggested to the housewife that zoning meant inspectors with other things than minimum yard sizes on their minds (see illustration, after p. 46).

The largest unified endorsement of zoning in Houston came from those areas where any student of the subject would expect support to originate: the middle-income, post-World War II subdivisions, those suburbs within the city. Lacking the glue of status and money to enforce their covenants, they watched the intrusion of scattered commercial uses into their areas. They still believed their single-family homes worth saving but they lacked the means to do so independently of municipal help. In zoning they saw the chance for municipal assumption of responsibility.[4]

To this observer the most noticeable physical distinction between Los Angeles and Houston lies in the residential area. In Los Angeles, serious about its detached, single-family areas, the medium-price, single-family residential subdivision has managed to maintain its residential purity far better than its counterpart in Houston. This is precisely what zoning can do best. This, in turn, explains why the planner, looking for the grand things in Houston, good and evil—the shopping center, the strip development, blight on the fringes of the central business district, the impact of expressways on adjacent land—ignores or overlooks that radio repair store in the $12,000 house.

The experience of these communities suggests that there is no "conservative" viewpoint on zoning. The citizens of Winnetka and Parsipanny who use zoning with alacrity probably hold virtually identical views on other social and political issues with their counterparts in Ogle County and Houston who fought zoning as an alien technique.

THE LIBERAL AND ZONING

Lest citing examples of the ambivalent approach taken to zoning by conservatives creates the impression that political libertarians hold some consistent views in this area, I hasten to correct it. One can begin with Rye, one of the larger suburbs of New York City.

The City Council, composed exclusively of Republicans, was listening with sympathy to developers' proposals to erect apartments and row housing. In an election year the Democrats struck back:

> We believe the type of row housing that the Planning Commission supports will seriously alter the nature of our community. This type of structure can be found in Baltimore, the Queens and in the Bronx —communities very different from ours. We see no reason why Rye should add apartment-type buildings by down grading zoning requirements—Rye should remain a community of individual residences.[5]

In Washington, D. C., the residents of single-family homes on the northwest side have battled for years against an influx of foreign embassies. In 1963 the Russians sought permission from the zoning board to convert a sixteen-acre estate near the Maryland border into an embassy. Opposition from the neighbors was, as might be expected, intense. The zoning board was composed of five persons, two of whom were government employees. The board granted the Russian petition by a 3 to 2 vote with both government employees in the majority. The neighbors brought suit in the District Court, alleging that the State Department brought improper pressure on the government employees to grant the petition. The court agreed:

> If nothing else, these two Board members were made to know that a favorable decision would be pleasing, and an unfavorable decision displeasing, to persons in very high governmental brackets. . . . The pressures were not crudely or indelicately exerted. There was no threat or command. There was no promise of reward. But the pressures were nevertheless real, and the Board members contacted could not fail to be aware that they would incur administrative displeasure if they decided the appeal unfavorably.
> In the vernacular, which is always more picturesque and frequently more expressive than legal jargon, this insidious approach is known as the "soft approach" or "soft touch." I therefore conclude that the *ex parte*, secret contacts here were of a character which deprived plaintiffs of a fair and impartial hearing.[6]

In 1963 my associate, Fred Bosselman, and I wrote an article, "Suburban Zoning and the Apartment Boom."[7] We questioned the moral and constitutional validity of the efforts of many suburbs to use zoning to exclude apartments. Terry Sandalow, Professor at the University of Michigan Law School, wrote us that we were trying to foist "mid-twentieth century liberalism" on the suburbs. In a similar vein, Max Wehrly, the Executive Director of the Urban Land Institute, suggested that "the currently popular notion of planned heterogenity, which seems to be the present cult of the sociologist and others, is for the birds. It isn't what people want or around which they can best develop a continuing community relationship." Such sentiments came as a shock! If anything, Fred and I had worried that we had gone too far toward advocating a return to the baronial days of John Jacob Astor, when a man could do just about anything with his land except dig it up and dump it on his neighbor's.

THE MOTIVATIONS OF LOCAL LEADERS

Be he "conservative" or "liberal," the local leader believes, as I observed earlier, that when it comes to zoning he knows better than any professional. The significance of such a condition is this: more than in any other area of the law—including school administration—in zoning the layman is vested with the heady power of direct participation in decision-making, free of any centralized guidance or regulation. If he were always residing in Mr. Bassett's Shangri-La this might be an endurable situation, but in a society in which the quantity of land is fixed and the demands are increasing, there may be occasion to challenge the premises upon which this unrestricted lay control is based.

What motivates the local administrator or legislator in the turbulent field of zoning? Much of the shouting by local decision-makers is phrased in economic terms: the purported effect that development will have on the tax base. It is probably true, however, as some economists and planners have pointed out, that in the field of land use planning most laymen do not know or, indeed, care where their economic self-interest lies. Although one hears a lot of talk about the economic costs of large-acreage zoning or the ultimate tax consequences of the total insulation of the single-family home, the layman rarely bothers to analyze the economic consequences of the alternatives. When the female of the species shows up in hostile hundreds at zoning hearings and protests that apartments will overcrowd her schools, this phalanx of housewives is not primarily motivated by fear of added school costs. When the male revives sufficiently from his commuting and martinis to denounce at the hearing a so-called cluster development next to his traditional tract house subdivision, he is not impressed by figures which demonstrate that the cost of municipal services will be less than they are to service one more subdivision of rectilinear lots.

The resident of suburbia is concerned not with *what* but with *whom*. His overriding motivation is less economic than it is social. His wife spends more at the hairdresser in a month than the proposed apartment house will add to her husband's tax bill in a year. What worries both spouses is that the apartment development is a symbol of everything they fled in the city. When they protest that a change in dwelling type will cause a decline in the value of their property, their economic conclusion is based upon a social judgment.

An articulate developer in the East told me he can chart the reaction of the plan commission of any municipality in Westchester County to his proposal for a "cluster subdivision." (In the cluster subdivision the detached single-family dwelling on a separate rectangular lot is replaced by apartments, row houses or "clustered" detached dwellings, but the overall density is not necessarily increased because substantial areas of common open space are set aside for the common use of residents of the subdivision). The initial response is one of enthusiasm for the novel plot plan. It does have a catchy design. The local commissioner is as intrigued as he would be by four-color copy in an ad in the *New Yorker* magazine. The emotional empathy rises. Then there is a pause. This proposal represents people, not tonic water. The emotional graph levels off. And down it zooms as some practical soul asks: "What kind of nut would move to Wedgewood and not want his own backyard?"

Another citizen asks: "Well, if your costs are less, then, of course, you expect to reduce your prices?" With that the jig is up. It is apparent to all that the one sure result of this departure from accepted subdivision design is the introduction of persons who do not prefer life in detached single-family dwellings and presumably do not have social interests and attitudes in common with families now in the community. The double indictment is sufficient to counteract the most exquisite architectural rendering.

The importance of the social value is apparent not only in the attitude toward dwelling type. I have observed the same predominance of social impulses in the actions of local decision-makers on questions involving open space, discount houses and motels. In the exurbanite fringe of Chicago near Barrington and beyond, there live an increasing number of us who pay a considerable price in lost time and inconvenience for our devotion to open space. We join private hunt clubs, plant red pines by the thousands, subscribe to *American Forestry* magazine and—if no one is looking—may even send a few dollars to help the fight to "Save the Indiana Dunes." The catch is that we have not bothered to face the question, open space for whom? I recall the violent reaction from the residents of such five-acre minimum enclaves as Barrington Hills to proposals by the Cook County Forest Preserve to acquire 1,000 acres for public recreation. Not so long ago there came a tough rhetorical question from a McHenry County supervisor to whom I proposed a comprehensive reclassification of an exurbanite area from one-acre to three-acre minimum: "You characters," he said, "are always chanting 'open space.' Tell me, what will be the reaction of you and your space-loving neighbors if we decided to condemn 200 acres in Bull Valley for a County Forest Preserve?" I was tempted to ask him: "How would you like your daughter to marry a picnicker?"

It is not only we country folk who react that way to public open space, as New York's former Mayor Robert Wagner found out when he decided to approve the creation of a park on Breezy Point. The point was occupied by the Breezy Point Cooperative, a group of 2,750 middle-class homeowners, who kept a manned gate and a private beach. The thought of disturbing this privacy by the creation of a public park was enough to bring 4,000 pickets to march on city hall.[8]

Robert Wood in his book *1400 Governments* reminds us that this double standard is prevalent in Westchester County.

> Though exceptions exist among its municipalities, Westchester remains as someone has quipped dedicated "to zoning against Bronxification!" The stand against "Bronxification" consists fundamentally of policies designed to maintain reasonably low trends of density . . . outsiders have been excluded from the county's well developed park system. . . . "There is only one state park in this county, Mohansic, and Westchesterians don't particularly want any more. . . . They do hope, of course, that Bob Moses will build lots of state parks elsewhere to draw off the pressure."[9]

Similar fears lie behind the zoning treatment of motels in the suburbs. Motel is such a dirty word that the phrases "Motor Hotel" and "Motor Inn" have made their appearance partly as a response to the rather unimaginative attempts of communities to segregate motels from inns and hotels. The truth, as any college sophomore knows, is that illicit sex is just as rampant in hotels and probably more delectable at inns than in motels, but most suburbs do not have hotels and an inn has a connotation of snug respectability.

One of the most delightful vignettes of the suburban attitude toward the motel appeared in a case in which the client of a Chicago lawyer, Paul Black, charged a large suburb with unreasonableness because it denied him the right to build a motel in a zoning district where "hotels" were permitted.[10] The principal objection was that the motel was only a couple of blocks from the local high school. One witness for the village was the president of the board of education of the local high school:

> THE WITNESS: My opinion is that this would have a deleterious effect on the morals of the young people who are going to be required—
>
> THE COURT: On what do you base your opinion?

THE WITNESS: On the fact that this, or any motel or hotel, has a lot of transient trade which cannot be controlled. The students coming—

THE COURT: How would that affect the students?

THE WITNESS: The students coming to and from the school are generally believed by their parents to be under the control of the school.

THE COURT: How would that affect the students, is what I am trying to find out, if there is a motel there and the transients stop there. How will that affect the morals of the students?

THE WITNESS: Because I feel these youngsters could be enticed into this motel.

THE COURT: Enticed by whom?

THE WITNESS: By transient people.

THE COURT: Yes, go ahead. You mean the boys or the girls?

THE WITNESS: I think both, yes.

THE COURT: Both. And you think that strangers or transients will stand at the door and say, "Come on in little girl?"

THE WITNESS: Yes, I do.

.   .   .   .

THE COURT: Are you perhaps apprehensive about your children going into those places?

THE WITNESS: Yes, sir. . . .

THE COURT: Go ahead. To me, that is ridiculous. Go ahead.

The perplexed judge continued his questioning:

Q.: Do you have children?

A.: Yes, sir.

Q.: How old are they?

A.: I have a daughter 20 and I have a son 17.

Q.: The son is still of high school age?

A.: Yes, sir.

Q.: Well, let me ask you about your son. Do you think your son would accept the invitation of some dope addict to enter a motel room with him?

A.: Your Honor, I do not know. I would hope not. I do not think so.

Q.: Do you think your daughter, while she was of school age, would have?

A.: I do not think so.

Q.: Wouldn't that depend to a great extent upon what kind of bringing up the children would have?

A.: Yes, it does.

Q.: And those same children that you are afraid might be enticed into a motel, are children whose parents generally have not given them what you would consider the proper bringing up, is that right?

A.: Yes, I think that is correct.

Q.: So that it might not be the motel that would get them in. It would be the question of the proper bringing up at home that they did not have that would be responsible for it?

A.: I think that might be a part of the question, Your Honor.

And then this exchange which belongs in the How's That Again? Department:

Q.: Do you travel much?

A.: Yes, sir.

Q.: Do you get around to some communities where they have motels right in the heart of the city?

A.: I have traveled considerably in my job and I stayed in a lot of motels.

Another witness who claimed some experience in the study of juvenile delinquency for the Cook County Sheriff's Office was genuinely concerned about a motel because it would have an adverse effect upon public health. How?

THE WITNESS: By the spreading of venereal diseases and other things. I am quite familiar with that on the Board of Health.

THE COURT: Well, you can spread them in homes, too, can't you?

THE WITNESS: Certainly.

THE COURT: A motel does not spread the venereal disease, does it? You are more apt to get the disease from the result of sexual relationships from the back seat of a car where there is no running water

and no sanitary facilities to cleanse yourself than you are in a motel
where there are those facilities, is that right?

THE WITNESS: That's right.

Suburban attitudes toward the discount store display a similar
social bias. How different is the impact of a discount store on a
neighborhood from that of a Jewel Tea Store? The discount house
sells soft goods, offers a wider line of hardware, and probably it
attracts customers from a wider area because of its prices than
does its more conventional neighbor. But insofar as its "hard"
impact on neighboring residential uses is concerned—noise, traffic,
commercial character—I submit there is no difference, except that
we may not like to live in a neighborhood that includes a discount
house. I had a petition for rezoning in a Chicago suburb go up
in flames when, at almost the last minute, the client told me that
instead of a "Jewel Tea" store, Jewel intended to erect something
called a "Turnstyle." The description of this operation sounded
to me like a discount operation. I warned the client of the probable
change from public acceptance to rejection.

At the public hearing the witness for Jewel tried to be casual
about the plans:

> The present plan is to have this building house . . . our standard
> Jewel Food Store operation; adding to that the merchandise carried
> in modern self service drug stores as operated by a subsidiary cor-
> poration, Osco Drugs, plus an expansion of the merchandise line
> into other areas which are somewhat experimental with us as
> yet. . . .
>
> We are convinced that there is a real need and a future in self
> service merchandising beyond the scope of our present operations
> and it is our present thought that this will be a location for that
> new concept of merchandising.
>
> MR. BABCOCK: But would this all be under the management of Jewel
> Tea?
>
> MR. STURTEVANT: Yes, sir.

Then came the inevitable question by a member of the local
Board:

> In addition to Jewel food and so on, as you mentioned you stated

something about some other sort of merchandise. You are not referring to any discounting or anything like that, are you?

MR. STURTEVANT: We are referring to merchandising which is the subject of some discounting but I would not refer to it as discounting merchandise.

Because one objector was quick to pick up the idea, I asked the Jewel witness:

MR. BABCOCK: Now Mr. Cerveny asked, Mr. Sturtevant, if you might possibly merchandise clothes, garden supplies, auto supplies and towels. Aren't those items, in your opinion, that are also frequently found in separate establishments in shopping centers?

MR. STURTEVANT: They are. They are common to most drug stores now as well as to many food stores, as well as other types of merchandising.

MR. CERVENY: The reason I asked the question specifically on these things is because as I understand this new concept in merchandising which you refer to is primarily another term for what we also know as discount merchandising, and these particular items are the ones which are most susceptible to this kind of merchandising approach from those locations that I have visited.

I was amused to read of the identical reaction in a case arising in the suburbs of Philadelphia. The Curtis Hills Civic Association participated amicably through four years of hearings and negotiations as the local planning commission shaped the formation of John Merriam's 150-acre Cedarbrook development. The first apartment buildings were built without a fight, but when the shopping center began to go up and the neighbors found that its major tenant was to be a discount house instead of, as they described it, a "quiet type" operation, the civic association jumped into action with a lawsuit that went all the way to the Pennsylvania Supreme Court.[11] The opinion of the court notes: "[The opponents] testified they had no idea that a discount department store, as distinguished from a 'quiet type' operation, would become part of the shopping center. Had they known, it was urged, they would have opposed more strongly."

Now the heart of the matter is that all of us enjoy the services provided by public open space, motels, and discount houses.

But when we make use of them we feel either like a tourist or a cheapskate and neither of these words has acceptable social connotations. They carry overtones of rubberneck, cheapjack, or niggler. And we are delighted to indulge these desires provided we are not in our own stamping ground. Because we feel this way when we partake of these pleasures in other places, we certainly will not permit persons meeting that description to enter into our community. Professor Israel Stollman at Ohio State University put it this way.

> People, since they are people, always want to have their cake and eat it too. They are always containing within themselves values which are mutually inconsistent, but they haven't explored it enough to know they are inconsistent—they all have values which are in conflict with the sheer facts of life that an inch is an inch, a dollar is a dollar, a second is a second.

The same social root helps explain why the political segments of the metropolis are willing to forego their autonomy for joint operation and control of those municipal services which contain a minimum of social implications. We are the world's greatest innovators when it comes to sanitary systems, garbage disposal, and mosquito abatement. Storm water, tin cans, and mosquitoes have no overt social implications. Thus, a concession to metropolitan control in these functions really carries small risk to the important values. But when we suburbanites begin to pool our decision-making on residential density and housing type—on who is going to live where—then at last the economist will have displaced the social psychologist as the diagnostician.

THE PLAN COMMISSION: THE POINT OF ATTACK ON LAY CONTROL

There is among professionals—lawyers, planners, and, indeed, politicians—an increasing restlessness with the layman's power over land-use regulation. Recently this doubt has been directed toward the institution known as the plan commission. Alfred Bettman in 1935 questioned whether the plan commission would prove "in the long run" the best agency to administer land-use controls.[12]

My interest in this institution is directed toward its role as conduit or buffer between the professional planner and the local politician. In this role the plan commission has neither the training of the planner nor the political accountability of the legislator. The mayor of one large city in northern California put the politician's case against the plan commission this way:

> If there's going to be a political destruction of a good master plan it should be done out and aboveboard and at the place where everybody can see who the executioners are rather than through the planning commission.

The lawyer's frustrations were expressed in this fashion:

> We criticize the planner because he isn't a constitutional lawyer. But bear in mind these laymen don't know anything about either planning or constitutional law.

Another lawyer from the midwest deplored the reliance of local legislators on the planning commissions, "often an overrated institution anyway." Then the planner:

> You have two sets of judgments involved [in these planning decisions]. . . . The second set is the judgments of the planning commission which may not have gone to any school or read any book or subscribed to any publication but is simply reacting in an irresponsible political manner. Now, you have to give your elected politicians credit for being reasonably responsible politically, otherwise they're not going to survive. This does not follow for the planning commission and when it gets in the position of yielding to political pressures and overriding the technical judgments of (what we hope to be) a trained planner you've got a body which is neither fish, flesh nor fowl.

Or the articulate developer:

> The planning commission is the worst device that's ever been invented by man. . . . The councils will tend more—while they will listen to the screaming—they will also, I think, tend to listen to the pros. Our experience has been that councils are better than commissions. . . . The commission pretends to be a pro in a field in which there are pros.

It is my view that the plan commission, except, perhaps, in the smallest communities, is a dodo. It is, as a growing body of criticism suggests, neither expert nor responsible. It undoubtedly did make sense in the early days of municipal planning when well-trained professionals were scarce and pressures on land use were light, but today it is the principal deterrent to more meaningful communication between the professional planner and the politically responsible decision-maker. Planning should be as much a part of municipal staff responsibility, with direct accountability to the politician, as fire or police protection. One of the symptoms of the malaise that infects planning is the continued reliance on the part-time resident who serves on the commission. We worry about his qualifications, his background, his conflict of interests, and his lack of knowledge or political responsibility, but these problems are inherent in the assignment of this responsible function of local government to an unpaid, unelected, untrained citizen.

The professional, in planning or politics, has our respect, if not always our sympathy. We know what his benchmarks are likely to be. We understand the risks he must constantly weigh, the alternatives he must balance. He may disagree with us and defeat us, but generally we know why we were rejected. The same cannot be said of the inscrutable commissioners in their role as decision-makers.

We have been looking at the layman in his role as a decision-maker on behalf of the municipality, a public servant. The layman also may be cast against the public. The same individual who is determined to preserve the sanctity of the suburban way of life may also be the vice president in charge of land acquisition for a chain of supermarkets. The plan commissioner of Great Neck, Long Island may be the vice president in charge of development of Advanced Realty Development Co. The point is that in zoning the nonprofessional has a role as *private* decision-maker, and the intriguing ambivalence of our lay attitudes cannot be fully savored without a glance at the developer.

III

The Layman as Private Decision-Maker

"Certain rules, of course, are necessary in order to exercise some controls over speculative builders."

Victor Gruen

I T is commentary on the changes in our society that the layman
as private decision-maker is allotted only one chapter in a
book on the making of land-use decisions. Two generations ago he
would have occupied virtually the entire text.

But despite the multitude of rules which limit his action, the
private citizen is still the catalyst of most changes in the landscape.
Public construction represents less than half of total construction,
and private construction requires a private citizen with the initiative
to build. The public can plan and zone to its heart's content but
unless some investor is willing to build according to the plan there
will be no building. The history of zoning is proof of this, whether
one looks to the glaring examples of wishful over-zoning for industry or to the effective barricade to high density residential development represented by large lot zoning of the exurbs.

At the start a distinction should be made between the developer
in the industrial-commercial field and his home-building brother.
Each shares some common frustrations, and each deserves some of
the same criticisms, but the public attitudes toward the two types
are sufficiently different to suggest separate comment. If the suburban municipality expects nothing better than rape from the residential builder, her response to the industrial developer is more in

41

the nature of: "Chase me, I won't run far." Naturally, the reaction of the suitor varies accordingly.

Now that I think of it, the comparison of the relationship of the established community and prospective builders to the relationship of an eligible maiden and prospective suitors is not so farfetched. Many intangible factors affect the desirability of a particular suitor, but basically the lady looks for money and class. Similarly, a community looks first at the proposed builder from the standpoint of finance and social status. How will the builder's project affect the tax base? And foremost, what will be the social status of the people drawn into the community by the project?

Subject to a number of exceptions, the average suburban community believes commercial and industrial developers are desirable suitors while residential developers are not. The former usually add to the community's tax revenues more than they require in municipal services. The latter are popularly believed to add less to the tax base than the cost of municipal services they create, a myth which has been exposed by Ruth Mace in the book she edited, *Municipal Cost-Revenue Research in the United States*. And the community always suspects the residential developer of a secret desire to cater to the "mass market," defined as all social levels below that of the person using the term.

Because of this difference in municipal attitudes, the residential developer and the non-residential developer have in fact come to think of themselves as different. The residential developer, like the poor and lowly-born suitor, has had to sell his virtues to his intended mate. Success in this field comes to those who can best cover their product with a veneer of social and financial acceptability without actually pricing the product out of the market.

The non-residential developer, on the other hand, like the rich and handsome suitor, is more concerned with choosing a desirable consort than with persuading her to accept him. To the industrial developer success is measured by the size of the dowry. In the words of the old saying, he establishes very quickly what the community is: "Now, Madam, we are merely negotiating price."

Because the residential developer and the non-residential developer are in fact usually different persons whose success is measured on the one hand by salesmanship, and on the other hand by bargaining power, it is fitting that each group should be discussed separately, with exceptions to these broad generalizations noted as they appear.

THE RESIDENTIAL DEVELOPER

Few areas of our national scene have been subject to so much recent analysis, not all of it dispassionate, as has the housebuilding business. The debate over the character of this business is hysterical and confused. There is no consensus whether housebuilding is a homogenous industry or is part of a larger contracting and construction industry. Neither can the commentators agree whether the housebuilder is responsible for the frightful scene that confronts us or is simply a robot who responded to the commands of an inexorable nationwide demand. This uncertainty confuses the numerous charges against him.

Whatever the accountability of the housebuilder for the horrid landscape of our metropolitan areas, the public decision-maker, the suburban legislator or commissioner, knows that since World War II the man who has come before him with a subdivision plat is an entirely different species from the builder of the twenties and the thirties. The housebuilder in the fifties and sixties is more at home with the intricacies of double entry bookkeeping than with joists and rafters. He must comprehend the mysteries of federal mortgage policy, but he depends on salaried technicians to handle the problems of heating and insulation. He seeks explanations for the cyclical character of the demand for his product in variations in government fiscal policy and he pays economists handsome fees to explain the peaks and valleys. He underwrites costly research projects by suppliers to keep abreast of the technological changes in the housebuilding industry.

The decline of the small volume builder which began with the postwar housing boom has continued. A 1963 *House & Home* sampling showed that builders who started nine or fewer units a year made up 43 percent of the builders but accounted for only 2.6 percent of the volume of houses built.[1] An increasingly large percentage of new housing is constructed by publicly held companies such as Sunset International, Levitt, and Kaufman & Broad. The giants of the building industry—the builders of over 100 units per year who account for over 61 percent of total construction—are usually equipped with their own architects, engineers, and land planners. These combines are more aptly called land developers than housebuilders.

Unfortunately, many planners and municipal officials still picture the typical housebuilder as a fly-by-night character who tried housebuilding because he found the margin of profit too small in the "loan shark" racket. This is about as intolerable as picturing the typical Negro rolling drunks. In terms of the overall impact on new construction, the shoddy output of the disreputable operator is small in comparison to the product of the conscientious housebuilder.

In spite of his new sophistication, the housebuilder remains essentially a cautious animal. He should be, faced as he has been with substantial and complicated risks in financing, inadequate market analyses, quixotic twists in government housing programs, and a public image that would make a Jay Gould cringe. He is a calculating businessman who ten years before may have been an importer or stockbroker who sensed a fantastic new market. He cannot understand why his efforts to provide a supply for a new and obvious demand should be the subject of such widespread and emotional criticism.

Deservedly or not, the housebuilder is the popular villain in the sordid story of urban growth since World War II. A new devil's dictionary has been created to describe the condition of our metropolitan countryside. "Bulldoze" is a dirty word implying treatment of people as well as earth, "slurb" was invented to give a better word-taste of the dismal suburban scene than was provided by "sprawl," "picture window" is the favorite cliche of the amateur social psychologist, and "slummaker" is no longer an epithet reserved for the landlords in the central city. William Whyte, Jr. is correct: "Aesthetically, the result is a mess."[2]

Whether the housebuilder deserves the entire burden of responsibility is not only debatable but irrelevant. I have never understood the usefulness of the continuing attack on the developer for what he did in the salad days immediately after World War II. In 1963 an article appeared in *House & Home,* a better than average trade publication, entitled "The Albatross of Localism."[3] The piece attacked local zoning and subdivision regulations which hamstring the housebuilder. In response, Dennis O'Harrow, Executive Director of the American Society of Planning Officials, suggested that the developer remember that:

> it was the ancient mariner himself who shot the albatross and thus brought the necessity for using the bird as a neckpiece. Likewise, it was the developer, the subdivider, the housebuilder, who, because of his land butchery, shoddy construction practice and general irresponsibility made it necessary in the first place to devise building codes, housing codes, zoning and subdivision regulations.[4]

The response contains more poetry than relevance. Putting aside the historically incorrect suggestion that zoning was conceived as a response to the "general irresponsibility" of the developer, the comment has to it a quality of so's-your-old-man. It has about the same appeal as does the labor magnate when he retorts to criticism of his abuse of his present above-the-salt position by pointing to the blatant practices of industry in the nineteenth century.

Neither have I been able to grasp the logic behind the complaint that the developer is accountable to future generations for the incalculable and irretrievable loss of open space that has characterized metropolitan growth in the last two decades. Responsibility for this tragedy rests firmly upon the public decision-makers who were unwilling to spend the public money to acquire and hold that public asset. The most impressive and useful open space programs in this country have been the result of farsighted public action, such as the Cook County Forest Preserve surrounding Chicago, the Cleveland Park System, and Westchester County's Bronx River Parkway. If the public gets credit, as it should, for such masterpieces, it must assume the responsibility for the cases where it failed to act, and not try to cover its shame by pouting that the private decision-maker failed to set aside open space.

It would be just as meaningful to indict, as responsible agents, the fruit and dairy farmer and his local spokesmen in county government who could not, in the face of rising taxes, resist the capital gain in a sale to the promoter; or to lay the blame on Congress, which held out financial blandishments to buyers and builders through Veterans Administration and Federal Housing Administration loans. Why not nominate as candidate for devil the refugee from the city? He had no business pouring out into the fringes, and certainly he should not, by his abominable taste in housing, have encouraged the builder to desecrate our countryside.

During the last twenty years the builder sensed a chance to make money. In a period of enormous demand for housing it should surprise very few of his contemporaries that he followed the line of least resistance. As long as the demand stayed firm for the little boxes the residential developer did not have the slightest incentive to innovate. As long as the market was strong and the Federal Housing Administration equated the American Dream with an enlarged orange crate, the housebuilder would not touch a new idea. But the builder keeps a close eye on the market. As the sixties began he noted the steadily increasing vacancy and foreclosure rates in the houses he had been building. There was, he sensed, a marked shift in the market. Suddenly the market for low priced houses was glutted. Families reaching their thirties, traditionally eager purchasers of the tract house, were fewer because the depression had produced fewer of them.

At the other end of the spectrum, the old folks were growing more numerous and for them mowing a back yard had lost a good deal of its appeal. Many of them had money to buy or rent (to an extent that would have astounded their parents) if they could find the

Newspaper published by the Greater Houston Planning Association, an anti-zoning group (see pp. 27–28).

type of amenities they sought. There was even vague evidence that for some buyers, regardless of age or economic class, the status totem was shifting from the detached dwelling on the separate lot to something different, though no one could yet describe with precision what it was.

Whatever the explanation, history will show that the decade of the sixties was a time of climax for the housebuilder, an era of unpredictability and change in demand and one that carried the seeds of unprecedented opportunity and of failure. Unable to sell the product to which he had become accustomed, he found himself grasping for new ideas in the housing field and in the same bed with some strange avant-garde characters.

The same man who ten years ago was pouring foundations of bungalows with built-in barbecues and unfinished recreation rooms now is howling mad because a bunch of reluctant village trustees look suspiciously at his color slides which show what the Swedes have done with mixtures of row houses, high-rises and garden apartments interlarded with interior parks and common gardens. The smart developer now mouths way-out terms such as "cluster subdivision," "planned unit development," and "density zoning," and he is outraged that the municipality still regards the virginity of the detached single-family subdivision as worth fighting for. The builder who ten years ago would have gagged at the suggestion that he experiment with anything more novel than a curvilinear street plan is now dismayed that the local plan commission cannot comprehend either the economic waste implicit in their insistence upon half-acre lots nor the social importance of his proposals to introduce multiple-family dwellings into Maple Leaf Highlands. Or, in the place of the man who in 1950 was barely able to leaf through *The Homebuilders Journal,* the contemporary developer asks for a hundred reprints of a *Harvard Law Review* article on the legal basis for a zoning ordinance which permits a mixture of single-family, duplex, and row houses in the same zoning district.

The spread of our suburbs at increasingly lower densities of population has created economic and social segregation, as well as pressure on the financial resources of our communities and the taxpayers. This threatens not only the health and welfare of our suburbanites, but is to a large extent removing the base for local self-determination, necessitating increasing governmental interference and initiative on constantly higher and more remote levels.

Those words may sound like the conclusion of an interdepartmental committee of social scientists but they are the words of a very articulate and dollar-conscious land developer, Jerry Lloyd of Middletown, New York.

On February 7, 1966, David Bogdanoff, a well-known builder in the east, wrote the following letter to the Village Board of the Village of Briarcliff, New York, a wealthy Westchester County suburb, after a request for multifamily housing for elderly persons had been turned down:

Gentlemen:

Confusion still exists as to the proper role of zoning. In some of our communities it is held that land use should be directed towards servicing the housing, recreational and commercial needs, first of their people, and then, to the extent feasible, the needs of the County and of the region.

In others, as in Briarcliff, it is held that zoning should jealously guard those guarantees which the existing citizenry have written into the regulations. These guarantees are in the main:

1. That each newcomer must be wealthier than those who came before, but must be of a character to preserve the illusion that their poorer neighbors are as wealthy as they.

2. That the troubles of the world and of the market place must be excluded from the Village by the zoning curtain. Problems of the Elderly, of Open Space, of Population Explosion, of Civil Liberties, may be permitted for discussion in the school cafeteria, but they must not be allowed to confuse the directness of zoning policy which was established to preserve a haven of middle class euphoria set aside from the troubled world.

The Village Board of Briarcliff should be testimonialized for its steadfastness of purpose, its moral consistency and its high courage in its handling of the recent application for Senior Citizen Housing. . . .

But our Board has not gone far enough. Now that its fierce

courage has been demonstrated in keeping out the old folk, further logical and obvious steps must be taken to protect the future of the Village:

1—Since school taxes are much too high, public school privileges should be further regulated. In an R60 or in an R40 zone, only the first born of each family shall be eligible for public schooling. In an R20 or an R12 zone only one-half of the first born child shall be permitted. Apartments must send all their children to either private schools or to Pleasantville.

2—Public education shall end with the sixth year, and our present Junior and Senior High School building shall be preserved as an Historic Shrine.

3—No children shall be permitted to be born in an industrial, commercial, R12 or R20 zone. In an R60 zone, one child shall be permitted to be born every 15 years and in an R40 zone, one-half of a child shall be permitted to be born every 10 years. . . .

4—No funeral parlors shall be permitted in any zone, including the industrial, so that we need not be reminded of old age and death. No one, quoting our good neighbor, John Cheever, shall be permitted to die in any zone larger than R12.

5—End the nonsense of being part of Westchester County and of the State of New York. Briarcliff cannot afford their taxes nor share their problems. Briarcliff should accede from the State and the County and cease paying State, County and Judicial taxes. With our heroic Board in the leadership, we can go it alone. If the few Rhodesian Whites can face up to their overwhelming Negro majority, we, in Briarcliff, can face up to and rid ourselves of the State and County.

The five additional measures proposed above are a logical and necessary further development of the zoning policy so heroically defended by the Briarcliff Board's action in throwing out our mothers and our fathers and our uncles and our aunts. We must not rest on our laurels. From this first victory let us press forward to more and better zoning. From this Winter of our parents' discontent, let us fashion the Spring and Summer of a New and Younger Briarcliff.

The people of the Village and the members of the Board are well aware of my past and continued interest in the community. I hope and trust that they will feel free to call on my knowledge and experience in the zoning field to help draft the necessary legislation proposed.

The builder's motives today are no different from what they were twenty years ago: to make money in his chosen vocation. It just happens that today the builder agrees with the critics of his older models, but for different reasons. His professional critics look with horror on what the developer perpetrated twenty years ago because it offends their sense of aesthetics or public economy. The builder looks with distaste on what was done twenty years ago because it will not sell today.

But the house buyers of the 1950's are suspicious of these new ideas in housing, and as a practical matter they cannot switch their brand. One does not trade a house as easily as one might trade a car or switch breakfast cereals. The buyer of the tract house in 1951 is now a Village Trustee. He suspects that the potential buyer of a condominium or townhouse in 1965 is a denizen of the same urban jungle from whence he himself fled fifteen years ago.

The developer is hurt if he is charged with being a cheat because he proposes in 1965 to depart radically from the pattern of residential development he merchandised with such persuasion in 1951. The more sensitive developer realizes how shoddy, by today's demands, were his old ideas, and he cannot comprehend why the local plan commission and their constituents are not as prepared as he to accept change. After all, he is the same old Sam who in 1951 sold those homes they cherish so, only now he calls himself Samuel and has a strong bias toward the social and economic significance of housing development. He says local resistance to new housing ideas is uneconomic and undemocratic; the half-acre lot represents a frightful cost in public services; and consider all the city dwellers who still want to share the joys of suburban living.

And yet this same sanctimonious developer, now piously reflecting on the social unfairness and economic waste of suburbia's insistence of homogeneous tract housing, was twenty years ago promoting the tract subdivision with its forty-foot rectilinear lots in the name of progress and to "give our veterans a place to breathe."

The irony of the present debate over housebuilding is that the attack upon the builder's product of the fifties comes more from the professionals—sociologists, architects, and planners—than it does from those who occupy the builder's product. The attack on the housebuilding of the last two decades is directed not so much against the structural shoddiness of the product as it is toward the poor taste of the plat design and the wanton destruction of the landscape. If the builder's product was so disreputable, his sales pitch so flagrantly puffed, why, today, are so many thousands of his victims outraged when anyone proposes to destroy the character of their neighborhood by introducing a different style in housing? A clue to the causes of the current battle between the developer and the local resident who sits as a plan commissioner may be found in the fact that the misguided buyer of the developer's frightful tract house of the fifties does not resent his purchase. He resents rather any change in the design or type of the product, precisely the reform the professionals and the articulate developers now call for.

Whenever I hear a housebuilder say that he cannot understand why the suburbanites distrust his new ideas or why they continue to be delighted with the tract house sold them ten years ago, I am reminded of Mark Twain's archetypical con men, the Duke and the King, whose swindling was portrayed in *Huckleberry Finn*.

You will remember that the Duke and the King attracted about half the population of an Arkansas village by announcing that "David Garrick the Younger" and "Edmund Kean the Elder" would perform a "Thrilling Tragedy." The show actually consisted only of some nonsensical prancing by the King. The crowd immediately realized that they had been bilked, or, as they put it, "sold."

> Everybody sings out, "Sold!" and rose up mad, and was a-going for that stage and them tragedians. But a big, fine-looking man jumps up on a bench and shouts:
> "Hold on! Just a word, gentlemen." They stopped to listen. "We are sold—mighty badly sold. But we don't want to be the laughing-stock of this whole town, I reckon, and never hear the last of this thing as long as we live. *No*. What we want is to go out of here

quiet, and talk this show up, and sell the *rest* of the town! Then we'll all be in the same boat. Ain't that sensible?" ("You bet it is!— the jedge is right!" everybody sings out.) "All right, then—not a word about any sell. Go along home, and advise everybody to come and see the tragedy."

The other half of the town was also sold, and they filled the house on the second night. But on the third night the townsfolk planned their revenge:

> The third night the house was crammed again—and they warn't newcomers this time, but people that was at the show the other two nights. I stood by the duke at the door, and I see that every man that went in had his pockets bulging, or something muffled up under his coat—and I see it warn't no perfumery, neither, not by a long sight. I smelt sickly eggs by the barrel, and rotten cabbages, and such things; and if I know the signs of a dead cat being around, and I bet I do, there was sixty-four of them went in. I shoved in there for a minute, but it was too various for me; I couldn't stand it.

Today's housebuilder acts as if he expects the same third-night reaction. All these tract-house buyers were really "sold," he figures, and must be about ready to opt for something better. But to his surprise, he finds the customer really liked that entertainment, or else he's been kidding others so long he has convinced himself. He is throwing eggs and fruit not at the man who sold him the slap-stick comedy but at the man who wants him to switch to something more edifying.

The joy of a good laugh at the builder's expense should not obscure the fact that it is the housing consumer who suffers because of municipal parochialism. The consumer wants the product that the builder wants to build, but his desires are being frustrated by the municipality's exclusionary tactics.

The cause of these frustrations is so well known to builders and is so frankly acknowledged by local officials that an elaborate des-scription of their scope would be superfluous. Not a thwarted developer but a suburban official in New York said this:

> Unrealistic subdivision regulations, excessively rigid local codes,

needless delays in processing filed plats, political ineptness on the part of local planning officials, administrative personnel totally unfit in far too many instances for their technical tasks, citizen pressure groups which more often discourage responsible local decisions, fear of new land use concepts, hostility, distrust and many other weapons are regularly in use today to increase housing costs and effectively resist population growth in suburban communities.[5]

The technique of interminable delay has been elevated to a refined art by local decision-makers, so much so that the housebuilding industry has persuaded the legislatures in some states to provide by statute that a failure of a local body to make any decision on an application for final approval of a subdivision plat within a specified period of time shall be presumed to constitute approval of the development proposal. Even this is not sufficient to deter the ingenious suburban legislator. If by statute he must act on a final plat within sixty days, nothing in the law forbids a requirement in the ordinance of a tentative approval of a plat. With that ploy he can delay a decision for years without violating the law.

Delay is cost to the developer but it is not the only cost imposed by the municipality. Some of the more blunt among the municipalities demand that the developer pay $50 or $100 a lot as a grant-in-aid, so to speak, to the local schools or parks. The fact that the courts have usually declared this practice to be illegal does not deter the municipality: to the developer the payment demanded is probably not as significant, in cash or time, as the cost of taking the municipality to court. Occasionally the builder, faced with such dubious tactics, finds a way to calm his spleen if not eliminate this assessment. One builder in upstate New York had to pay the municipality fifty dollars a lot for "recreational purposes." He responded by including this amount as a separate and identifiable closing cost at the time of sale "much to the dismay of town officials who," according to the report, "are facing continual requests of new home owners for an accounting of these 'recreational purposes' fees."[6]

The most significant leverage enjoyed by the municipality, however, arises from the awareness on the part of the developer that he must deal with the suburb not just when he seeks approval of his plat but again and again for building permits, health code inspections, and at innumerable other levels of local regulation. Even the economically powerful developer knows that he may whip the municipality on zoning and still be beaten down in a dozen other regulatory arenas where he must face the village. The developer who is unwilling to compromise is either highly principled or in contact with a remarkably patient and generous financial angel.

The suburban municipality would prefer that the housebuilder just go away. Since the village cannot hope to bar him absolutely, it falls back on the ancient and proven technique of delay in the hope that, like the frustrated gopher hound, the developer will eventually give up and find himself another hole to nuzzle in.

Perhaps it is not so much this negative reaction which surprises the residential developer as it is the passion and rancor with which he is put off. He cannot comprehend how these folks, all of whom are as devoted as he to the free enterprise system, can regard him and his ideas as alien to the American economic system. Of course his antagonists do not dispute the principle; they just cannot accept the intermixing of money-making and the home. Most of them maintain a substantial distance between their particular market place and their hearth; and to them there is something unclean to the idea of making money out a place of abode. When to this legend there is added the residents' vague fear that some social change may be implicit in any novel proposal for residential development, it is small wonder that the developer is violently rejected when he tries to offer logic and economics as a basis for judging his proposal.

So the housebuilder moves on to the outer precincts of the metropolis where the Guernseys still outnumber the humans and where the farmer looks for an escape from his tax bind; or the builder makes deals and he compromises; or in rare instances he litigates, less in confidence of the outcome than in angry frustration. In a few inspired and well-heeled cases he literally builds a new town. More recently the builder turns to the professionals, the lawyers and planners, to draft legislation that will, in the name of social progress and economic common sense, save the suburbs from themselves.

Does all this mean that public control of land use should be abolished and the builder given a free hand? Jerry Lloyd would be the first to disclaim such an intent but it would not be fair to assume the following statement by Mr. Lloyd was mere rhetoric:

> It is ironic that this [urban] disorganization and sprawl should have been co-terminous with the very period in which urban planning has bloomed, in the number of practitioners, in the amount of funds expended and in the powers and means of control available. It is not unfair, therefore, to question whether planning is not partially a cause for our present troubles, rather-than merely a response to them.

I doubt whether the record of the housebuilder entitles him to such a show of confidence even by the most cynical observer of suburban practices. Because the critic questions the motives behind the suburban antagonism to the builder it does not follow that he must agree that the builder should be given a free hand to muck around with our housing and land. If we blame the greed of the local government and landowner, as much as the avarice of the builder, for our unhappy post-war landscape, it does not follow that the decision-making should be turned over to the latter.

What is significant and promising in the current revivalism on the part of the housebuilder is his identification with other forces that call for a reappraisal of the legal position of the municipality in the land use field. The developer now finds himself aligned with professionals whom he formerly regarded as nuts (and who looked upon him as some form of vermin), and he adds a down-to-earth quality to the attack on the absolute presumption of municipal sovereignty in land-use planning. The housebuilder in the sixties may be the brigade in reserve whose arrival may reverse the contest, in the legislatures and the courts, in favor of the metropolitan

interests that the more sophisticated suburbs have so far success-
fully resisted.

THE NON-RESIDENTIAL DEVELOPER

For the non-residential builder, the discussion with the municipality usually starts from the premise that he is wanted. In some
cases the municipality throws itself at the developer's feet, offering,
if not gold, at least the equivalent in land, tax relief, and financing
of the plant. Even in those instances where the municipality is
prepared to bargain, the debate relates not to whether the plant
should enter. The issues relate to the design of the buildings, the
plot plan, the landscaping, the impact on vehicular traffic, and the
appropriate "buffers" to protect any neighboring residential development. This circumstance contributes to a more rational dialogue
than in the case of proposals for residential development, if that is
saying much. In place of highly charged exchanges over schools,
children, transients, and "character," as is the custom on residential proposals, the industrial developer will more often find
himself faced with demands that he redesign the layout of his site
to provide greater amenity. This posture at least has the advantage
of emphasizing in the zoning debate the role of the architect, landscape architect, or planner rather than the role of the housewife.

Out of the haggling between the industrial developer and the
public decision-maker, the developer may be persuaded to invest
more imagination (as well as cash) in design to make the industry
a better neighbor without significant penalty to the function of the
building. This is in marked contrast to the results of the haggling
over residential development that often force the developer to
abandon imagination and style for dreary conformity as the price
of permission to build.

There is, as I suggested, an exception to this contrast between
the zoning debate over non-residential and residential development
proposals. The exception reflects the extension of the social fears
of the municipality over proposals for new ideas in residential development. The middle-class suburb often rejects industries which

would employ large numbers of lower-class workers. Anyone who doubts this need only request a rezoning on behalf of an industrial developer to whom land is merchandise to be marketed to a variety of buyers. Unlike the identifiable corporate buyer who seeks rezoning for a specific purpose underwritten by a specific corporate image, the merchandiser of industrial land rarely can pinpoint the eventual user. More than once I have sought rezoning for industrial use only to be asked the precise purpose for which the property will be used if it is rezoned. My response is that the land will be used for any one of the many uses permitted under the municipality's industrial zoning classification and will be subject to that zoning. This invariable invokes the "yes-but" response, "We know you will comply with the regulations of our industrial district but *which* of the many uses permitted under our M-2 regulations will occupy the site?"

It is useless to observe that the inquisitors drew the ordinance and they must have concluded that the various permitted industrial (or commercial) uses were compatible and equally acceptable. You do not win votes by pointing out to the public decision-makers that their *ad hoc* inquiry amounts to an impeachment of their own preestablished regulations. In many instances this frustrating line of inquiry has its roots in an ancient ordinance which is so loosely drawn that it does, indeed, permit industries with unsavory characteristics that would threaten neighboring property values.

More often one suspects that back of the demand for identification of the specific industrial use is a fear bottomed on a social nervousness. I encountered this attitude in litigation in Des Plaines, Illinois, a large suburb of Chicago, when my client, a railroad, wanted some excess land rezoned for industrial use but could not identify the eventual buyer. A planner called as a witness for the city explained his reasons for opposing the rezoning:

> For police protection. All of us know by reading the papers what goes on many times of people who work in factories, people who have no roots, who are of the rougher type of individuals, and they do not belong in a locality where there are children running around,

school children. So from the standpoint of morals and safety, it is dangerous to have an M-2 classification on the subject site.[7]

A Michigan attorney and counsel for a number of municipalities, expressed the same fear to me this way:

> We have a local community here . . . and they have a zoning ordinance which covers an area of several hundred acres owned by the Chrysler Corporation. This was purchased with the intention of building a research center. It's my understanding that this property is zoned for single-family dwellings but the city would welcome Chrysler's entrance and it will change the ordinance to satisfy the Chrysler Corporation. But the hypocrisy is that the land is still zoned for single-family purposes. . . . What is done is to maintain the single-family classification and as each prospective developer comes in they size him up. . . . The idea is that they would for example welcome the Ford Motor Company because it's solvent but we don't want Joe's XYZ Company because they may fail and we don't want that sort of thing. In other words you are getting through your zoning ordinance a sort of super-regulatory body over the type of industrial enterprise that will come in. This is certainly outside the police power.

Some suburbanites go so far as to oppose any industry whatsoever for fear of its social implications. In one Chicago suburb where such fears run high, a local property owners' group sent out a newsletter opposing the village administration's proposed rezoning of a large vacant tract of land to Office and Research. "You know what *Office and Research* means," they said, "it means more *Multiple-Family.*"

In another wealthy Chicago suburb some years ago a local grocer wrote a letter to the City Council requesting permission to put two employees to work in his back room preparing lemon juice concentrate. The Council's minutes report that it instructed the Village Clerk to write to the merchant informing him that the zoning ordimade no provision for manufacturing.

With these occasional exceptions for "lower-class" developers courting "high-class" suburbs, the industrial and commercial developer finds himself much in demand. There is, however, an air of unreality in municipal expectations about industrial development, and this is particularly noticeable in the fancy zoning attire donned by many a municipality in the hope of attracting the non-residential developer. The elaborate provisions in many suburban ordinances for the "Office and Research" District represents a hypnosis with labels rather than a concern for reality. If something is tagged "research" it has an air of modernity and no other qualifications for development seem necessary although the "research" may involve testing jet engines or new techniques for manufacturing varnish. The pell-mell rush of suburban municipalities to adopt "Industrial Performance Standards" without bothering to analyze their substance and their application to the facts of the particular suburb is another illustration of the wishing-may-make-it-true philosophy which confronts the developer. I recall the bemused reaction of one promoter of industrial real estate who, upon examining the industrial performance standards of a small suburb of Chicago, discovered that its performance standards for industrial noise and smoke were less restrictive than those in the heavy industrial district of Cook County. But, by golly, the village did have industrial "performance standards!"

The enchantment with the tag "Industrial Park" is another case of self-mesmerization. The municipality may not have sufficient water and sewer facilities, or streets designed to carry industrial traffic, but it has 100 acres zoned "Industrial Park."

The truth is that for the industrial buyer, whether promoter or a corporation looking for a branch plant site, the condition of the local industrial zoning is far down on the list of significant factors. In some cases this is because the buyer would prefer to take an option on land zoned residential and take the minor risk of a rezoning. He can buy the residential land at a lower price than if it were already blessed with an industrial classification and his local advisers assure him that the village, hungry for jobs and revenues, will accede to the rezoning. More often this indifference to zoning on the part of the industrial buyer rests on nothing more than a far greater concern with other factors. The availability and ade-

quacy of public utilities, transportation facilities, the local tax policies, the labor market and topography of the site, and even its
cost, are what count. Climate generally ranks ahead of satisfactory
zoning regulations.

The industrial developer or corporate buyer knows that as long
as he is within generous boundaries of acceptable development
(which might exclude fertilizer plants and canning factories) he
can usually obtain whatever rezoning he needs for his particular
purpose at his desired location. If zoning is a factor to the industrial buyer, more often it is the residential zoning in the area rather
than the industrial zoning that matters. The industrial buyer is concerned with adequate housing for both management and labor.
He will be sufficiently sophisticated to examine the types of residential zoning in the undeveloped areas of the community to satisfy himself that the entire spectrum of demand for housing, both
in cost and type of dwelling, is available.

The industrial developer may not be impressed by the particular
zoning classification of his favorite site but he is not indifferent to
the quality of planning in the community. I use "planning" in its
most comprehensive sense to embrace fiscal, economic, and physical development. When the industrial realtor or land buyer for a
corporation inquires about the quality of public services, the adequacy of recreational facilities, and the availability of adequate
housing and transportation, he addresses himself to the substance
of the public planning program in its most catholic sense. The irony
is that this message is precisely what professional planners have
been trying to get across to municipalities for three decades: that
planning is a sustained program of municipal development in the
public and private sectors that involves something more than col-
oring a variety of geometric designs on a zoning map. I expect
this message will come through more persuasively from the industrial buyer than it has from the professional planner.

I spoke of the quality of planning in the *community*. I did not
use the word *municipality*. The distinction between these two words
is another area in which the voice of the industrial developer will

contribute to more intelligent planning. It is an area where the planner has been hesitant to speak out to his municipal employer or client; namely, the imperative need in the field of land development for municipalities to think beyond their haphazard political boundaries. A "community" in the economic and social context is not, in most cases, the same as a municipality, and it is the quality of the former that is important to the prospective industrial buyer. To the corporation and the developer of commercial facilities, the significant development factors generally extend beyond the boundaries of the particular municipality in which the industrial site is located. Unlike our laws which treat the municipality as the sole public decision-maker in many areas of planning, the industrial developer knows that many of these issues are not capable of being resolved in such a fragmented context. His concern with transportation, recreation, and housing requires that, except in the most isolated locations, he must evaluate regional conditions. This wide horizon on the part of the industrial developer may contribute to a broader-gauge vision toward these problems on the part of our local duchies.

IV

The Planner

> "Oh, I am a cook and a captain bold,
>   And the mate of the *Nancy* brig,
>   And a bo'sun tight, and a midshipmite,
>   And the crew of the captain's gig."
>
> > "The Yarn of the *Nancy Bell*"
> > W. S. Gilbert

As a member of the legal profession which has thrived on the slings and arrows of public comment, not all of it friendly, I assure the planner that these few rubber-tipped darts are an omen of future economic wellbeing.

Here indeed is the schizoid. The layman may believe zoning is a good thing or an abomination, depending on his role; the lawyer may ignore it; and the judge may be overcome by ennui. The planner does not know what his attitude is or should be. The condition is not surprising when one understands that many planners are not certain what manner of animal they are themselves.

The reasons for the general neurotic state of the planning profession are not hard to identify.

ZONING AS A CAUSE OF THE PLANNER'S VERTIGO

We begin with the dismal fact that the planner, whether consultant or staff member, finds that he must spend more time working with zoning than with any other planning tool; zoning, the very device he has been taught in planning schools and professional conventions to regard as a dull, ineffective instrument. If you spent

75 per cent of your time working with a system you had been taught to scorn, it would indeed drive you—or any self-respecting professional—to plans for the year 2000. John Delafons put it right:

> The first obstacle [to more coherent and effective use of land controls in America] is the impatience of many American planners themselves with the whole system of zoning, which many of them seem to regard as an incubus to be thrown off before there can be any real progress in planning. . . . It would help matters forward if the academic planners would take more interest in these practical matters.[1]

The more articulate and the more sensitive the planner, the greater is his embarrassment with zoning; the greater his inevitable professional humiliation that to the layman zoning *is* planning. He feels a compulsion to apologize—between reports to his commission on requests for rezoning.

Why do planners spend so much time with zoning? A Pennsylvania planner gave his opinion:

> I suspect that certain of them just feel more comfortable doing that. I think planners, certain of them . . . just like their rut. . . . They like to know when they come to work today there aren't going to be any new problems or new issues to face. I'm going to settle down to that comfortable old zoning ordinance and review five applications today for a change in zoning and make a recommendation on it. See?

This syndrome is evident among almost all planners whatever their professional emphasis. Zoning is infra dig not only to the planner who has the background of the social geographer and to the avant-garde type who has brought planning into the computer parlor, but also to the planner who emphasizes design and hence is understandably frustrated by the rigid bulk controls of traditional zoning. In their strident criticism of the stifling impact of traditional districting on design, these brick worshipers forget that it is not districting that is important but what we believe to be the consequences of districting: certainty and objectivity in the legal rules which control the affairs of men.

The planner would much prefer not to be bothered with zoning. This is apparent not only in his conversations but in his journals and his convention agenda. The reader would never know from a review of the *Journal* of the American Institute of Planners or the agendas of the AIP conventions that there was a device called "zoning." The *Journal* is addicted to such exotic subjects as "Early Mormon Community Planning," "The City Symbolic," or "Images of Urban Areas: Their Struture and Psychological Foundations," and "An Evaluation of the 'Choice' Theory of Planning." It is up to the profession to choose the subjects for professional debate and a concern for historical precedent is healthy, but the profession can expect to appear precious and self-conscious by snubbing the one subject which must occupy its time on return to its offices.

THE PLANNER AND HIS CLIENTS

There is a second reason for this dizziness among the planners. The common denominator among all professionals is their function as counsel to their clients, patients, or parishioners. The state of a professional's emotional health is directly related to the extent to which his counsel is accepted by his principal, a subject over-worked by those who scrutinize the psyche of the Protestant minister. In this context the city planner has more frustrations in common with the Congregational preacher than he does with the doctor, the attorney, and the engineer. Unlike his counterparts in law, medicine, and engineering, the planner has no sanctions by which to enforce his opinions. "Those of us," one California planner explained, "who are working in this field oftentimes find that it is the decision of the bank or something that really makes or breaks a project."

The client may not relish the lawyer's advice, but when counsel cites a precedent as controlling that generally settles the matter, if not in conference then in court. If the doctor infers death or disability as the alternative to following his advice, the unhappy patient accepts surgery or therapy, however distasteful the prospect may be. The debate over the use of the Golden Gate Bridge as an artery of the new Bay Area rail transport system was immediately silenced by the advice of the engineers that structurally the proposal was unsound.

The planner, unfortunately, can only invoke history, a feeble threat to municipal clients who believe they, too, can read. Not only does the planner's client believe he is equally qualified to interpret the tea leaves, but he is also comforted by the knowledge that in mid-twentieth-century America he can flee his suburban or urban nest if the planner's predictions of rot come to pass. This pleasant alternative is not available to the diabetic or to the defendant in a lawsuit.

The intolerable position of the planner is underscored by his suspicion that the final decisions will not be his. He suspects that too often he will be a reluctant mouthpiece for local prejudice. The planner's frustration is vented in his favorite dictum: "Zoning is negative." This, by the way, is one of those half-truths which is a convenient substitute for thought. If the effective resistance of Westchester County to what Robert Wood refers to as "Bronxification" is negative, I ask, what is positive? Hugh Pomeroy told me during the last decade rezoning to larger minimum lots in Westchester County has reduced the theoretical maximum population by one million persons. If two-thirds of the residential land in the New York metropolitan area is purposely zoned for half-acre or more density, I do not understand the meaning of "negative." Nor does it make the maxim less inaccurate to suggest that zoning is negative because it is "against." To the suburban resident zoning is not against, it is *for*. *For* low density, *for* high-cost housing, *for* socially homogenous communities. I sympathize with the suburban resident who insists that his community's zoning policies are no more "negative" than the selective urban renewal practices of his urban municipal neighbor. I believe it was Bill Wheaton of the University of California Institute of Urban and Regional Development who said that a city does not hire a planner until it decides it does not want anyone else in the city.

Fred Bair suggests that the sore of planning is that planners do not know what they are doing, or that they are trying to do too much. Try this, for example, as a definition of professional responsibilities that embraces everything and says little:

> first, the planner investigates, describes, synthesizes, analyzes and evaluates the overall problems and conditions of the urban area;
>
> second, the planner predicts or estimates changes and trends, evaluates needs, considers alternatives and recommends practices for action by his community client.

That is from the "Statement on Responsibility of the Planner" published in October, 1962, by the American Institute of Planners.

I believe the condition of the profession is more dismal than suggested by Bair. The planners do know what they are doing and the intelligent ones are appalled: they are, too frequently, being used by their municipal employers.

I do not suggest that the planner cannot be a sophisticated spokesman. Without peer in this category was beloved Hugh Pomeroy, mother hen to Westchester County's suburban chicks. What his suburban employers did not learn from Hugh on how to equate low density with "general welfare" is not teachable. (I like to believe that after four years of Hugh's presence St. Peter has established the first heavenly minimum half-acre district.) Hugh was called frequently to act as an expert witness in zoning litigation. Adversity on the witness chair seemed to invoke his best, as Hugh's contretemps with a federal district judge in Detroit testifies. In *City of Ann Arbor* v. *Northwestern Park Construction Corporation*[2] Hugh was testifying on behalf of the city in opposition to a proposal to rezone residential property for a shopping center. Hugh had been testifying for a half hour in his incomparable fashion:

> THE COURT: (interposing) You admit the country is being built up without your exclusive supervision?
>
> A.: Oh, I should say, and done very well, by many people.
>
> THE COURT: I am glad to hear you admit it.

A.: The first essential attribute of a planner is a degree of humbleness, your Honor.

.   .   .   .

THE COURT: (interposing) Why don't you wait until somebody asks you a question.

A.: I haven't completed the answer. Part of the answer has transgressed. I am sorry.

THE COURT: I am glad you recognize it has transgressed, and transgressed badly.

MR. FAHRNER [city attorney]: Mr. Pomeroy—

THE COURT: (interposing) It is one of the faults of letting a witness run with a bit in his mouth.

.   .   .   .

THE COURT: (interposing) Well, please. I don't have to listen to this, do I?

MR. FAHRNER: Not if you don't want to, your Honor.

THE COURT: Well, I suggest that we stop somewhere, because when this man comes all the way from Westchester County and is telling the administrative agencies of the City of Ann Arbor as to where they have jurisdiction and where they don't I think he is going far afield.

I appreciate the fact that he is a very humble witness, but I think he is exceeding his field here.

.   .   .   .

THE WITNESS: May I have the question read?

THE REPORTER: (reading):
"Q.: [by Mr. Bonisteel, plaintiff's attorney] Do you know what the needs of the people are in Ann Arbor? Did you make a determination of that?"

A.: Needs with respect to what?

Q.: General living conditions.

A.: Do you want it answered in exactly those terms?

Q.: Did you make a survey to that effect?

A.: As to the general living conditions of the people in Ann Arbor?

Q.: And their needs.

A.: Their needs would have to deal with housing, with recreational facilities, with libraries, with all sorts of things. If you will tell me what kind of needs you mean, I will try to answer it. The question is ridiculous in its present form.

THE COURT: Don't characterize the question as being ridiculous. You just try to answer him. It isn't for you to evaluate anything here. You are produced here as a witness, and you are proving to be a difficult witness on cross examination. Under our system of justice, why, the opposing side has the right to cross examine, and it isn't considered to be even good taste for a witness to characterize a question as being ridiculous.

THE WITNESS: May I ask what the question means?

THE COURT: Well, that is different. If you don't understand it, why, that is completely within your prerogative. But don't characterize anything around this Courtroom as being ridiculous, because this is not a ridiculous proceeding.

THE WITNESS: I asked first for an explanation of the question and was castigated for asking it. Now, may I ask for an explanation of the question, if you want an answer. I am not trying to play with you. I want to get the facts on the record.

THE COURT: I want to assure you that you can't play with him so long as I am supervising the conduct of this trial.

You can imagine Ann Arbor lost before Judge Thomas Thornton. On appeal, the decision of the trial court was reversed. Hugh Pomeroy generally came out on top.

Undoubtedly there were times when even Hugh Pomeroy had to swim upstream against his municipal client's desires. The planning profession would deserve more respect as a profession if it hailed such independence of spirit and criticized those of its members who are noted only as naive and dissembling puppets.

Other planners can be equally forthright and candid on behalf of their client's policies. I offer you a second example of a professional justification for suburban exclusionary zoning. This exchange took place between the court and a planning expert in a Maryland case.[3]

[THE COURT]: Mr. Rogers, I'm sorry to have brought you back. You may consider this a minor matter but to me it's a rather important factor in the case. I wanted to ask you what is your definition of general welfare?

A.: Your Honor, I would define it this way: The general welfare in relation to the zoning and planning aspects of the state's police power would relate to the depreciation of property holdings as caused by land use of an individual property owner, would relate to the question of the impact of the land use of an individual property on the existing uses of surrounding property.

Q.: What do you mean by welfare, if you eliminate the health, safety and morals?

A.: Then I come back to my first point, which is welfare in terms of the effect of land use, such as R-6 and R-10 [minimum residential lot area of 6,000 square feet and 10,000 square feet], on existing land use in the community and the effect of this on the cash, whether it appreciates or depreciates the property values of the community. And under those two points I think it is the first point that is valid here: that this tends to break up the unity of this community which exists now; it tends to insert into this community, in effect, a pimple of a different density. But also, it is a different economic group, a difference of community interest; and all these things tend to create a different community in an island of a different sort.

Q.: Economically, you mean people of less means would come into the community?

A.: I think obviously that is true. I don't mean this quite in the sense of class distinction, though. I do mean it in the sense of community interest. Where you have a community interest, to be honest about it, there are sometimes class elements involved; but basically it is economic values. In our own population people are moving up and down as well as horizontal. It seems to me it is a wise plan to recognize this as a part of general welfare. And the community should be kept up as a community and the people should be able to move in and out of this community in terms of the interest they have in coming into the community.

Q.: That would be in the way of a recognition of certain economic class distinctions. Is that correct?

A.: I think that is part of it, yes sir. I don't think that is the basic part, because if you take Mr. Jones in 1930 he may be part of an R-6 community of interest you might say. And in 1940 he might be part of an R-20 community of interest. And in 1950 he may be back in R-6. So it is not a question of freezing people in a class; but it is a question of providing a whole spectrum of facilities to suit every economic class in this country. Now rightly or wrongly, there are economic classes.

I admire that candid evaluation.

THE BOUNDARIES OF THE PLANNER'S RESPONSIBILITY

There is a third explanation for the planner's split personality. He has gnawing doubts about the correct limits of his professional responsibility.

This uncertainty is frequently evident in his equivocal role in planning administration. The planner is not happy with his ambiguous posture in planning administration, a condition which is underscored when the community has a lay plan commission. I will not labor the point except to note that in England there has been considerable public debate (e.g., letters to *The Times*) over the ethical responsibilities of the planner who disagrees with the decisions of his lay commission. In this country many staff planners are increasingly disturbed by the frequent conflict between their responsibility to the plan commission and their ultimate accountability to the elected officials. On occasion I have felt obliged to subpoena a staff planner where I knew local objection to my client's request was not endorsed by the professional. It is not a pleasant experience, either for the witness or for the lawyer who respects the courage of such professional independence.

This uncertainty is even more the case on substantive issues where his advice is sought. Here is one case in point.

The planner has serious doubts, as well he should, on the part competitive economic consequences should play in zoning decisions, but increasingly this issue is present when proposals for commercial development require rezoning. Viewed from one perspective, it is none of the community's business whether the developer is an economic fool and ends up in bankruptcy. Neither is it the function of zoning to protect existing business from technological obsolescence. If the proposed shopping center passes the usual tests of neighborhood compatibility and acceptable vehicular facilities, public and private, and meets meaningful design standards (a virtue too rarely demanded), the matter should be settled. Whether the development will contribute to the debilitation of the central business district or will shortly share vacancies with another center within a half mile is not, it is said, a legitimate purpose of zoning.

Walter Blucher, planner and lawyer, has made the point with his customary incisiveness.

> Now I'll give you another example of how futile zoning really is: I was in Kansas City, Kansas, which by and large has pretty good planning. . . . Well, in Kansas City before you can get a zoning change for a shopping center you've got to bring in a market analysis. And I went out and looked at six sites for proposed shopping centers out here and just on the basis of the information I could get from the Plan Commission I reached the conclusion that this total area could support three shopping centers. They asked me what they should do.
>   "Grant all six," I said. "Only three will survive—but grant all six. . . . How can you determine which three they ought to be? . . . I have no objection to converting some supermarkets into recreation centers—when some of these supermarkets go busted. There is one thing that you might be sure of—that these are so built and so located that no matter what happens they will not impinge badly upon the surrounding area. In other words, you've got to see that things are planned so that traffic doesn't come through—so that they don't hurt. Once you've done this thing, you've done your part in zoning."
> Well, this was a practical answer, I suppose. Was it from a planning standpoint a sound answer to say that we're going to zone for six shopping centers in an area which will support only three? I don't know.

I asked Robert Leary, former Planning Director for Ann Arbor, Michigan (whose municipal client was attempting to manufacture pep pills for an anemic central business district) whether he had faced this problem.

> We have [a shopping center] on the east right now—I think about 85,000 square feet of enclosed area which is under construction; and we have another one of about 175,000 square feet under construc-

tion on the west side of the city—both are inside the city—and a third one proposed—it's in the process of annexation, and the development plan is on the desk—and the question of zoning is facing the council. When it faces the council it faces us. We have been rather torn by what you might call conflicts of interest because we have been retained by the Chamber of Commerce jointly with the city council for a $32,000 study of the central business district—what's wrong, what should we do? The planning commission has recommended the development of the shopping center on the east side, the one that's on the west side, and we're in the process of studying the third, which will also be located on the west side. Now we're getting a reaction from the downtown merchants who are questioning our loyalty and our motive. Are you just mouthing support for downtown while doing your best to tear it down as soon as possible? And we had to get up and make ourselves heard on this subject. First of all, a shopping center—as we have told them—is a valid part of the land use and, irrespective of its location inside or outside the corporate limits of the city, is going to have a very definite impact on the downtown area. We believe that shopping centers are pretty much in the category of death and taxes—they're inevitable—and that a properly controlled shopping center within the corporate limits of the city, is better for the city, generally,—the community, generally—than is a shopping center possibly not adequately controlled on the same location, let's say a quarter of a mile from the city limits.

Even those planners who frankly admit they consider economic impact reveal a concern. One West Coast planner admitted: "Well, I think it is legitimate and we have made many plans based on the premise that it is legitimate, but it's the one thing which causes me more sleepless nights than anything else we do."

The planners are correct in their concern over the definition of their responsibilities. Their reluctance to use zoning for economic planning places them in the mainstream of American policy. The planner, nevertheless, is troubled by his reluctance to exercise judgment in economic areas. There are at least three reason for this schizophrenia. The planner senses that it is somewhat anomalous for him to gripe that zoning is negative or—as Blucher put it—"futile," and then to refuse to endorse zoning as a weapon in economic planning. He may be right in his reluctance but the fault is not in the potential of zoning, about which he is so critical, but in the planner's unwillingness to advocate the full potential of this tool in the economic sphere.

The second reason for this troubled conscience is that the planner knows that, in other contexts, the economic impact of land-use policy is an accepted consideration in planning and has, indeed, become respectable in the eyes of some courts. It is modern zoning practice to forbid gas stations and other drive-in facilities in "prime retail" business districts, although there are a substantial number of preexisting gas stations which consequently enjoy a legal shield against additional competition. The rationale is that the intrusion of more gas stations will have an adverse impact upon retail, pedestrian-oriented facilities in the business neighborhood. The community has a valid interest in the maintenance of a viable shopping area. Presumably too many gas stations will discourage shopping; business will fall off, vacancies will increase, tax values will plummet, and the revenues needed for public purposes will be dissipated. Planners will suggest that the community does not "need" any more gas stations and there are omens that this argument will receive sympathetic response from the courts.

Precisely the same public policy arguments could be advanced in opposition to the proposed second shopping center that threatens the central business district or the competitive shopping center, but they are less likely to be accepted by courts than in the case of gas stations and taverns.

The village of Edina, Minnesota, a suburb of Minneapolis, ran into a judicial buzz saw in 1960 when it made the error of candidly admitting that its action in rezoning property for "office buildings" in the Southdale Square development and refusing to rezone for a shopping center was based upon an intent to protect a neighboring shopping center.[4] A report on the Southdale property to the Edina Plan Commission by its planning director, George Hite, was put in evidence. Included in Mr. Hite's report was the following statement:

The Southdale Square development then with its emphasis on convenience goods and personal service facilities is therefore *non-competitive* with the regional retail center which emphasizes "comparative" or "shoppers" facilities. This distinction is important when considering the objective of developing *non-competitive* adjacent land uses.

The judge held the action of Edina unlawful and found:

That the only logical, plausible or reasonable explanation for the action of the Village . . . is a belief on the part of the governing authorities of said Village that it is within their province, under the state statutes authorizing zoning . . . to protect the businesses surrounding the plaintiffs' property from competition.

The Court finds . . . that the policies and philosophy of zoning of the Planning Engineer of the Planning Commission of the Village of Edina, in the matter of limitation of competition, have dominated and controlled the action of the Village . . . with respect to the zoning of the Pearce property.

Perhaps the Village of Edina would have done better to dissemble a bit, to talk less of economic considerations and talk more of the customary zoning factors of neighborhood "character," traffic patterns, and existing nonconforming uses.

Whether the courts or planners approve, there is no doubt that zoning is often regarded as a convenient and intentional device to limit competition. A few years ago the Detroit retail gasoline dealers petitioned the Detroit Common Council to revise the municipal zoning ordinance to prohibit any more gas stations. In 1957 the Chicago Independent Grocers' Association, whose members sell package beer, endorsed an amendment to the Chicago zoning ordinance which allowed nonconforming grocery stores to remain in residential areas but provided that taverns in the same districts would be eliminated in seven years.

The planner recognizes that each time he makes decisions on the location of commercial areas he is conferring potential benefits upon some and denying them to others. The fact that under zoning this result is inevitable does not lessen the planner's sense of doubt. Said one planner:

I know I hold two views simultaneously about this, which are opposed views. I feel that it's not the business of planners to interfere or meddle in the process of selecting who happens to get rich, whether the getting rich is by selling land or the getting rich is by developing land with a shopping center or something else. And I don't think it's proper for the planner to take into account the need for protecting an existing and established business—to say we're not going to give you the zoning you want because we want to protect the existing shopping center. Nor is it the place of the planner to say we are going to give you the zoning that you want because we think you're a better guy than the existing center. This is not an area in which planners should meddle. Now the other view I have which conflicts with this one is this: it is the business of the planners to influence the decision of how much land, over-all in the community, is going to be devoted to commercial use or any other given use, and it's also the business of the planners to influence what the locations of these uses are going to be. Now what's hard to reconcile is, how do you go about influencing these two important decisions without affecting the relationships among individual landowners. And I don't see any clean-cut way out of the dilemma except one of pursuing a very tight ethical course and leaving yourself as blind as possible to the personalities and identities and affiliations of individual property owners, and when making recommendations to zone or don't zone to consider only how much land there's going to be in a zone classification, is this the right location, does the design fit its neighborhood, and so on.

Any self-enforced blindness to economic consequences that the planner may try to adopt when dealing with commercial uses seems to disappear, however, when he turns his attention to residential districts. Here he must devote his efforts to protecting the existing investment in a "way of living."

When a planner finds it necessary to justify his municipal client's determination to exclude apartments from areas dedicated to the single-family house—even when apartments will not increase the number of dwelling units per acre—he cannot invoke the traditional arguments advanced against high-rise apartments: that they increase density and, purportedly, raise the costs of public services. In the case of a cluster subdivision, where dwelling units are grouped but no increase in density results, the only plausible argument in opposition to the departure from the detached dwelling pattern is the maintenance of the "character" of the detached dwelling neighborhood. The use of public regulation in such a case to provide this protection to the single-family area must be justified on the ground that a change in character (intrusion of multiple family) will have a direct, substantial, and adverse impact on property values. This rationale should sound familiar to the established shopkeeper who watches with fear the rezoning of nearby land for a new shopping center. Unfortunately for the small merchant, the values which enjoy the overt protection of traditional zoning regulation are residential values, not commercial values.

I debated this paradox with a planner (P) and a judge (J) of a state appellate court. I guess Babcock (B) came in third:

B.: Is there any possible conflict between your views on multiple coming into the single-family area and the right that the single family have to be protected, and your views on commercial uses where the existing commercial doesn't seem to have the right to be protected. Is it just because one is a castle and the other is business?

J.: Oh, I think there's a distinction.

B.: You said before that the "atmosphere," which I read as property values, a way of life in the single-family neighborhood, is entitled to protection from this intrusion, even though all the 'hard' standards have been met. But now I gather that the little pre-existing shopping center did not have a legitimate right—

P.: There is a vast distinction between what—

B.: I'm always suspicious when you start out with an adjective like 'vast.' It's like the lawyer who says "obviously."

P.: But I do think there's a distinction between the two kinds of protection which we are talking about. In the one instance we are protecting a residential community against the intrusion—as you said, the intrusion—into its neighborhood of uses which are going to be one next to another.

B.: Stop there. Now this guy who is already here with the shopping center couldn't care less about this new commercial use unless it represented an intrusion into his neighborhood.

P.: He's not concerned with the intrusion into his neighborhood, as neighborhood. He's not concerned with the relationship of this shopping center to his physically, but he is concerned with the intrusion, economically—

B.: So the interesting result we may have is that something much less tangible than property values is entitled to protection. However, something as tangible as a property value, namely the existing shopping center, is—

J.: Is not necessarily. I think I maintained very clearly before that it wasn't the property value as such. To me, the property value drop with the multiple-family coming into the residential is evidence of the interference with the value that I wanted to protect. It is evidence of it.

B.: You wanted to protect a way of living.

J.: The property value is evidence of the fact that you're interfering.

B.: I want to protect the way of living for this little business, here.

P.: Now here again we're faced with these mixtures of motives and mixtures of values. As in the case of the residences, we said that we are not going to protect the residential man. We are not going to protect him from the intrusion of different people. Different people come in; he doesn't like it. That's too bad; they come in. This is a conflict and clash of peoples, perhaps, but we are neutral on that score. We are going to protect him insofar as his concern is reflected in the physical pattern of his area. Single-family dwellings exclusively or not. In the case of the businessman, I think to protect him from another competing businessman would be on the par of protecting white people from Negro people.

B.: To the contrary, I think you might analogize the residential protection to the race question, but not the commercial.

P.: One deals with—one set of analogies deals with social and economic competitive questions and the other deals with physical questions of design.

J.: The businessman is not objecting to the physical form of the buildings that are going to come into his area. Nor is it going to change the nature and character of the neighborhood. It's going to change the methods and manners of carrying on business.

B.: But why should I have a stronger case if my only objection is to the physical design as against the case when I object because it will affect my economic values? Is my objection to the way that building looks entitled to a stronger position than my objection to whether or not I survive economically?

P.: That is precisely the way I'm putting it. And I think this is the way the cards stack right now. And I don't know, but I think if I thought it through I could conclude that maybe this is the way the cards should stack. Because it's part of our system and part of our society, and I think properly so, that we don't say to a businessman that once you're in business you've got it made—we're there to protect you. You have risk. Personally, I think it's unfortunate that the good old-fashioned word, risk, isn't liked by business anymore. I think that we cannot have the kind of economic society we have and we want to have without risk. And it is this element of risk, including the risk of a competitor who comes in and takes your business away because he has a better location—he chose better than you did; or he has more design—he was imaginative or hired more imaginative architects than you did; or—

B.: But you wouldn't extend this risk to my living.

P.: That is right. I want to protect you against that kind of risk because you're not engaged in business where you sleep. This is a completely different area of social concern.

B.: Why should we protect them from risk socially but not protect them from risk economically?

J.: Because I think you're getting off the point.

P.: It's on the point. It's on the point to this extent, and it actually, I think, gets to the heart of all of the issues we could possibly discuss, and that is what is our total set of goals as a society? It's conceivable that if we knew enough about them, and despite the spate of books on goals in America we don't know enough about our total goals. If we knew enough about them we might find that one or two or more are head-on in conflict with one another, and if we lived long enough we would find we couldn't live with both of them simultaneously. But in any case we do have a set of social goals with respect to our economic state of life. We have a set of social goals with respect to our residential way of life. And the things that both things have in common, even though apparently they're in conflict, is that in each case we are setting out to protect our established goals.

The planner, of course, was right. There is no paradox if we recognize that the apparent conflict in our attitude toward the respective functions of zoning in residential and commercial areas derives from two American objectives that remain viable in spite of suggestions by economists and sociologists that our national ambivalence makes these objectives more legend than fact. These objectives are protection of the single-family home, and protection of the free market place. In land-use policy, the first objective requires that government take positive action, the second demands that the government refuse to take positive action.

PLANNING AS A PROFESSION

I have been offering my suggestions why the planner is in such a professional tizzy over zoning. One dominant impression is that the planner really is not sure what he is or what he wants to be. Unlike his brothers in medicine, law, and engineering, he not only does not have a defined status, he is not himself able to provide a definition. Is he a sociologist, an architect, a geographer, a landscape architect, a land economist? Or, more accurately, is each of these a "planner" because he deals with design or with land values, demography, or social ecology? Perhaps the current uncertainty is no more than an obvious reflection of the profession's youth. (The planner can rejoin by citing the time when barbers were surgeons and laymen sat on appellate courts and he will point to the current disputes between the bar, on the one hand, and accountants and collection agencies on the other over their respective professional spheres of influence.) There may be inherent in this inconstant art of land-use planning a vagueness which repels a precise definition of the qualifications and responsibility of the practitioner. This open-ended condition may be beneficial for the rest of the community that does not always appreciate the smug fraternities of law and medicine, but it denies the planner the sense of apartness which is a major factor in the confidence of other professions.

The current debate within the profession over the value of state registration is indicative of the planner's doubts. While the planners argue among themselves, more cohesive groups such as engineers and landscape architects seek and frequently obtain legislation in this area that not only will frustrate the planner but will be inimical to the best interests of a society which should encourage and profit from as broad a background as possible in those whose judgment we seek in setting land-use policy.

The planner's neurosis is not made happier by the treatment he receives from other professionals. If the planner pretends to deal with design he encounters the scorn or, worse, the indifference of the architect. One architect put the case bluntly:

> The future of planning and architecture alike depends on understanding the profundity of Le Corbusier's simple statement: "Architecture and urbanism are in fact one problem only and are not separate questions. They demand one solution only and this is the work of one profession only."[5]

When historian Lewis Mumford questions the overemphasis on the role of cement in planning he does not, however, direct his fire at architects but, if you please, at the planners:

> As the inner life of the Greek city disintegrated, the outer aspect of the city showed a far higher degree of formal order and coherence. Certainly, the Hellenistic city was more sanitary, and often more prosperous, than the Hellenic city. If it was more severely regimented it was also, to a superficial eye at least, more beautiful. Not the city of the sixth and fifth centuries but that of the third century, would be the modern town planner's dream: not the city of culture but the city of commerce and political exploitation: not the city of free men but the city of insolent power and ostentatious wealth.[6]

One can hardly blame the planner for being incensed. Why should a historian accuse him of design bias when he has been bluntly advised by the architects that urban designs is none of his business!

Let the planner venture an opinion on the impact of a particular development on urban land values and the economist challenges. Says the University of Wisconsin's Professor Richard Ratcliff:

> We see the city planner as the interpreter of the market-expressed preferences of consumers, not as a mystic who knows better than the consumer what is good for him. . . .
>
> There are too few people well trained in this highly complex process [of planning] and too many persons in responsible positions who lack an understanding of basic city growth principles and who give major weight to engineering considerations or to aesthetic values or who view urban design as an esoteric art incapable of understanding save by the elect.[7]

The planner can respond that the difficulty is not that the planner lacks an understanding of "basic city growth principles"—whatever they are—but that the planner's principles are not the same as those of the economist or the real estate developer.

It is hard enough to be crossing swords simultaneously with architects, land economists, and engineers. When the planner must at the same time be *en garde* with the lawyers he cannot be blamed for viewing himself as a modern D'Artagnan at the top of the castle stairs. The clash with the lawyers could be the most serious, at least for the planning consultant whose success depends in large part on the preparation of comprehensive plans. When a community hires a planner to prepare a plan it expects not only a guide to future growth but implementing legislation, usually in the form of zoning and subdivision ordinances. Since the Standard Zoning Act of 1925, private planning consultants have made a good living drafting zoning ordinances. The fact that in the last two decades most planners insist that a comprehensive plan should come first does not lessen the significance to the municipal client of the implementing ordinances—the here and now of planning—that are part of the package. It is in this area that the planner has been charged by the bar with engaging in the unauthorized practice of law.

In Illinois the Committee on Unauthorized Practice of the Illinois State Bar Association has been swatting at planning consultants up and down the state. The dialogue was bound to become somewhat acrid when the Committee, in 1960, observed: "the public's interests are not well served when a technician well-versed in one field attempts to draft a paste-pot-and-scissors ordinance by patching together bits of zoning and land use law from other cities and possibly other states."[8] The planning consultant has responded to this attack. Instead of calling his work a "Zoning Ordinance" he will tag his rose with some name such as "Proposed Planning Standards for Zoning Districts" and on the lower right-hand corner of the cover he will note: "Legal Review by State's Attorney for ————County."

The bar may appear stuffy about its cherished prerogatives, and it may be charged with seeing the public interest in its own image. However, it requires a professional cohesiveness such as is displayed by the accountants or credit men to negotiate treaties with the attorneys, and this is a characteristic absent from the planning brotherhood. It is easy to sympathize with the planner without overlooking his responsibility for the present unhappy condition.

For years the planner regarded the lawyer as totally inadequate to converse about city planning. The lawyer was either uninterested or, through his commitments to private clients, too interested, to be of value in the drafting of local land-use regulations. I frequently sense that when the planner protests that the bar is not interested (i.e., not qualified) in planning he is verbalizing a subconscious fear that the bar intends to take over a significant part of the professional consulting work involved in planning. Both professions patently have a necessary role in counseling on land-use development. Until the planner achieves a status which provides him with a feeling of professional security, he will display a self-consciousness in his dealings with the bar.

THE PLANNER AND THE COURTS

The judge sees and hears the planner in the latter's capacity as an expert witness. The encounter is not always empathic. When the highest appellate court in New York State upheld by a 4–3 vote the constitutionality of the amortization (gradual elimination without compensation) of uses that did not conform to the zoning regulations, the dissenting opinion was caustic.

> We are now told that the protection of nonconforming uses in the beginning [of zoning] was a stratagem of city planners 'prompted by a fear that the courts would hold unconstitutional any zoning ordinance which attempted to eliminate existing nonconforming uses.'
>
> .   .   .   .
>
> Zoning, like other public programs, is not always best administered at the hands of its enthusiasts. The existence of nonconforming uses has spoiled the symmetry in the minds of zoning experts.[9]

I sense a growing skepticism on the part of the courts toward the usefulness of the planner as a guide to a rational resolution of a land use dispute. Ironically, this does not derive only from the expected source: a conservative judicial reaction to the phrase "comprehensive planning," such as that expressed by Pennsylvania's Chief Justice John Bell:

> Planning is not, as some zealous advocates believe, something new. These proponents talk and act as if it were something as novel as the science of space, and they as wise as Solomon. Planning is as old as the hills. Hannibal, Alexander the Great, Genghis Kahn, Napoleon, Wellington, Washington, Grant, Lee, Eisenhower, and nearly all the great Generals of history planned their campaigns and battles. Business men plan in advance their inventories and future business; every great doctor plans a serious operation; every able lawyer plans the trial or argument of important cases; housewives plan their meals and their day. Nevertheless, planning has become a fetish which in too many instances is carried to extremes, with little or no consideration given to the constitutionally ordained rights of property owners, or to the possible lack of judgment and vision of the temporary planners.[10]

There is an increasing judicial suspicion that planners, at least the private consultants, drift where the wind blows strongest. This attitude is in part attributable to the limited number of planning consultants available to testify as expert witnesses. Their repeated appearances as experts, first on behalf of a community, next on behalf of a developer, breed a judicial reaction that the man is a professional witness, not a professional planner.

I recall the experience of one lawyer before the supreme court of a midwest state. The abstracts and briefs had been distributed to the justices and the attorney was about to commence oral argument. He had not made much progress before one of the justices broke in with the observation that the printed abstract of the record before the trial court appeared to be incomplete. Counsel was nonplused, not knowing whether the supposed omission was due to some error by the printer which had eluded him or whether the point was more serious—that a significant issue had been ignored at the trial level. In any event, the attorney responded as equivocally as he could, hoping for more enlightenment. He got his answer with a laughing eye. "No, counsel, as I look at your index of expert planning witnesses I do not see Mr.————'s name among them." The judge referred to a planning consultant who frequently appeared as an expert witness. With that the rest of the bench smiled.

As a symptom, this incident is disturbing. As I have talked with judges on appellate and trial courts I have sensed that this reaction is not diminishing. This is, of course, not the fault of the planning profession generally (which has wrestled from time to time with a definition of the planner's ethical responsibilities as an expert witness), any more than the tendency of some orthopedic surgeons to spend more time in personal injury litigation than in practice is characteristic of the medical profession generally. Parenthetically, the orthopedic surgeon-witness has one advantage over the planner-witness: each personal injury case is tried before a new jury, while most zoning cases are bench trials and the decider (the judge) can remember how frequently the same planner shows up in his courtroom. I have tried to mitigate this problem by calling in planners from other parts of the country, thus providing a new face for the trial judge and a fresh name on appeal. Then I must hazard a cross-examination which will emphasize the limited acquaintance of the witness with the locality. This is the way the attorney for the plaintiff started his cross-examination of Hugh Pomeroy, in the *Ann Arbor* case I referred to earlier:[11]

Q.: Mr. Pomeroy, when did you first come to the City of Ann Arbor?

A.: My first visit to the City of Ann Arbor was twenty years ago.

Q.: How long did you stay that time?

A.: Just passing through.

Q.: I see. And when was the next time you came to Ann Arbor?

A.: Last November.

Q.: Is that the first time you have been in Ann Arbor—how long did you stay that time?

A.: My testimony will indicate—

Q.: (interposing) Just answer.

A.: Two days.

Q.: How much?

A.: Two days.

Q.: What days were those?

A.: Saturday and Sunday, as my testimony stated.

Q.: I see. And when was the next time you came to Ann Arbor?

A.: As my testimony stated, last Sunday.

Q.: So you have been in the City of Ann Arbor two days, and then you came just prior to this lawsuit; is that correct?

The debasing of the planner's coinage before the bench is not easily halted. Some planners follow a policy of testifying only on behalf of municipalities. If they disagree with a municipal decision they will refuse to testify on its behalf but they will also refuse to testify for the developer. This may be salve to a sensitive conscience but it gives the appearance to the bench that the witness assumes all virtue is on one side (a point opposing counsel will bring out immediately on cross-examination).

The education of the bench requires a judicial awareness that in the planner's judgment the appropriate use of each parcel of land can only be determined in relation to the land use of surrounding parcels and in the context of the particular community in which it is located. The planner may, with a most secure conscience, testify on Tuesday in support of the location of a shopping center at Point A in community B, and reappear on Thursday to oppose a shopping center at point Y in community Z. The planner would be advised, however, to avoid too many generalizations about the importance of shopping centers generally in the first case and restrict his observations to the particular location.

The inherent characteristic of most planner-witnesses is their reluctance to stop talking. This may be due to the fact that planners, unlike engineers or orthopedists, lack precise yardsticks and so feel a need to elaborate. This tendency, by the way, makes the articulate and shrewd planner a difficult witness to handle on cross-examination. I have often found that my own witnesses do better when cross-examined than they did for me on direct—not, I add, a comforting observation. The truth is that if the lawyer follows the catechism never to ask a question on cross unless he knows what the answer will be, he would never ask a planner a question which requires an opinion response.

I emphasize this growing judicial skepticism because it arises not only from a distaste for planning on the part of property-oriented judges but also from those members of the bench who are sympathetic with the appropriateness of public participation in decisions over land-use policy. It is to these latter judges the planning profession must look for understanding and encouragement. If that part of the bench becomes disenchanted, planning is going to be discredited in the one area where it should be endorsed.

Hence the malaise of the planner: a pervading ennui with zoning, the most prevalent tool in planning; an absence of effective sanctions by which to enforce his professional advice; deep uncertainty about the appropriate limits of his responsibilities; and, if this were not enough, direct and often effective attack by other professions. To use the terminology of the sociologist, the planner's role in society is unclear both to him and to those with whom he must deal. He needs time to develop the rules and traditions that will bring him a sense of professional security.

V

The Lawyer

> "For the lawyers, they write according to the states in which they live, what is received law, and not what ought to be law."
>
> Bacon

JOHN Delafons offers this inscrutable British comment about the origins of zoning in the United States: "All the great luminaries of the early days of zoning were lawyers—Edward Bassett, Alfred Bettman, James Metzenbaum, F. B. Williams. Given the nature of American institutions and attitudes, it may have been inevitable that lawyers rather than architects or professional planners should have been the successful pioneers of land-use controls."[1]

Whatever may be meant by the "nature of American institutions," it is true that lawyers dominated the early days of zoning. This preeminence of the lawyer in the early days was not, however, as significant to the course of zoning law in America as was the legal profession's notable lack of interest during the following three decades. It was as though the bar regarded the initial victories for zoning in the United States Supreme Court and the state courts in the twenties as an intellectual exercise. Having demonstrated their facility at the game, the lawyers tossed the cards to onlookers to play with as they chose. From 1930 to 1950 the bar—and in that I include municipal attorneys—regard zoning as a piddling bother. This indifference of the bar was matched by the indifference of most law schools toward the legal and social implications of land-use planning. Zoning had an inheritance of constitutional law and real property law, but neither parent wished to admit responsibility for parenthood. As a result, zoning and city planning were orphans in the law school, disdained by constitutional law professors as unworthy and dismissed by teachers of real property law as simple toys of the real estate brokers. The early texts on zoning law were written by such practitioners as Bassett, Newman Baker, Frank B. Williams, and James Metzenbaum, all of whom had learned the law of zoning by helping to make it. Understandably these men were interested more in the practical aspects of making zoning work than in the broad social and economic overtones.

As the body of precedents in zoning and planning law has grown, the faculties of the law schools have taken an increasing interest in the subject. Today virtually every one of the leading law schools has on its faculty at least one teacher who specializes in land-use law and who regards it not as an odd corner of the law of real property but as a matter of significant public policy. This change is not, to be sure, a cause but a result of the national concern with an acceptable resolution of the conflict between a fixed supply of land and an exploding population.

Whatever the role of architects, planners, and economists, the ultimate resolution, as well as the day-to-day contests, will be legal. Because the major issues in zoning are no longer petty but embrace major social and political implications, they are attracting some of the legal brains which otherwise find their meat in debate over the fiduciary responsibilities of corporate management, or in the resolution of the bargaining between labor and capital.

The awakening in the law schools is having its impact upon the law student as he emerges from the campus to the bar. I have encountered scores of law school graduates seeking experience in land use planning because of an interest derived from school. These young lawyers will make their impact on the bar only gradually as they work into positions of responsibility. But if the interest of the current crop of lawyers is translated into continuing interest there will be plenty of articulate advocates practicing in this field in the seventies.

For the present, however, the attitude of the practicing bar toward zoning is one of repugnance. John A. McCarty, a member of the Boston Bar, whose experience with zoning has, it appears, not been entirely pleasant, writes:

> It seems to be an inescapable conclusion that, as matters now stand, the zoning law, far from accomplishing its purpose to protect the property rights of others, has become merely an instrument of special favor, under which those with power or influence can either by special permission or by change of zoning, accomplish their own selfish purposes, regardless of the overall public good.[2]

While some attorneys believe that the flaw in zoning is that it is too susceptible to change, other attorneys like Paul Black of Chicago dislike the system for contrary reasons:

> The indictment in zoning today, at the local level, is that it is approached with hysteria, not reason. Much of the day to day workings of zoning bodies, and the decisions which flow from their hearings and deliberations, is a result of what is popular, not what is right . . . zoning abuse is defined by zoning zealots as *any* relief given *any* applicant from the harsh terms of the ordinance. As a result, a "suburban neurosis" or sensitivity developed toward the granting of zoning relief.[3]

The result of these moods is strikingly different from that produced by boredom, the earlier response of the bar. The latter attitude produces indifference; the former is bound to produce reaction, either toward reform of this irresponsible area of the law or toward condemning it out of hand. To speak of the bar's distaste for zoning is to invite the challenge rightly directed at any generality, but I believe most lawyers who have had occasion to practice in this field will accept the fairness of the characterization.

The reasons for this attitude vary and I will not do more than identify a few. We cannot dismiss the continuing influence of the attorney who is against any efforts by the community to limit the choices available to the landowner. He reflects the general distaste of his clients for any form of governmental regulation, as well as his own distaste at having to practice a legal specialty which did not even exist when he went to law school. To him, the attempt to regulate anything but junk yards and trailer camps is clearly unconstitutional. He may find himself on the same side of the brief in a zoning case with a civil libertarian, but our property-oriented brother, like Jane Jacobs, just happens to reach the right conclusions from the wrong premises.

The more disturbing protests against current zoning practice come from lawyers who recognize that government does have a legitimate responsibility to set guidelines in the market place for the allocation of land uses. The most frequent protest is that zoning administration in its modern dress seriously impinges upon procedural due process. These lawyers assert that the lengthy hearings and complicated procedures involved in zoning are merely hypocritical devices set up to exhaust the potential developer and force him to come to terms with the arbitrary wishes of the local leaders, whether these terms be the compulsory dedication of a park or a school land or arrangements with the proper people. This group is fond of speaking of the "leverage theory" of zoning; the use of the zoning ordinance as a basis for bargaining by the municipality. A midwestern lawyer described how this works:

> If they ever start taking us to court—we do a lot of things down at the Planning Commission we can't do under the law. But we don't tell them that. We put restrictions on them and say you have to have a setback of 100 feet here and so forth—usually you can work it out with them if you're pleasant and they realize you're interested in keeping the value of the land up. This is what you'd call the leverage function of a local zoning ordinance. So we've been really frightened that if they ever really start taking us to court, we're sunk.

These fears of local discretion run wild are not only the concern of those lawyers who represent the property owner. This condition weighs upon the lawyer who represents municipalities. While he may be less strident in his protest, his doubts cut deeper because of the conflict between his professional conscience and his responsibilities to his client.

David Craig, Director of Public Safety for Pittsburgh, and an outstanding authority on the law of zoning, expressed concern for the tendencies, "A general prevalence of particularized zoning is taking us away from predictability and anonymity. The increasing propensity for the examination of each proposal as it comes up appears, on the surface at least, to go counter to the idea of planning the development of the community in advance."[4]

Did I say attorneys for municipalities are more cautious in their comments? Not Robert Michalski, City Attorney, Palo Alto, California:

> Many planning commission hearings have taken on the character of an oriental bazaar where applicants wheel and deal with the commission on conditions and restrictions to be imposed on zoning. Some hearings are more like the ancient circuses in the coliseum of Rome in the days of Nero except that the Christians then got a better deal from the lions than some applicants do from the planning commission. Now instead of thumbs down or up the planning commissioner asks for show of hands. Too often decisions are not based on facts or master plans, but on pressures of bitterly complaining or approving neighborhood improvement associations who are coming out from every rock, packing council chambers and snowing commissions with petitions. The protection of health, safety and general welfare has been forgotten in the desire to control competition, keep out foreigners, favor special interests, obtain public right of way for free, zone tax users out and high tax payers in.[5]

It was a planner who spoke the language of the lawyers when he said:

> It's not districting which is so essential, but what we imagine to be the consequences of districting. . . . The certainty, the objectivity—these are the important things. And if we can accomplish them without the districting, then districting isn't the important thing. . . . And what we're doing when we invent the floating zone and the this-gadget and the that-gadget is to try, some way, to accomplish some vague kind of flexible land use pattern that we long for without abandoning the certainty and objectivity that we want to keep. . . . And there is this danger also, that all these gadgets in turn are abused just as much as districting was abused. In fact, they lend themselves much more readily to abuse.

The lawyers themselves are not immune from the disease of "neighborism" which infects the layman when he takes on the role of municipal decision-maker. One Ohio lawyer put it this way:

> I have seen so many councils and zoning boards which are arbitrary—even though I'm supposed to be representing them in most cases. I feel that so many of these questions are decided on emotional bases. Neighborhood feelings. I have one councilman who has been on the council in————for 20 years. He's a lawyer. His father was the leading municipal bond lawyer in the city for years and years. And I've heard him say over and over again that on zoning questions he will vote for or against the zoning change based solely on the wishes of the people in the area. The neighbors. The neighborhood. He makes no bones about it.

There lurks in many a lawyer a sneaking suspicion that the substance and procedure of zoning as practiced in most of our suburbs today is a violation of somebody's constitutional rights.

Another aspect of suburban zoning that disturbs even the lawyer who is sympathetic to planning is the accumulating evidence that the device is being used as a technique to keep out all but the elect. I do not refer to the more obvious if less demonstrable charges by a few zealots that zoning is a dandy tool to promote racially-segregated neighborhoods, although I recall one instance where Robert Ming, a Chicago lawyer, appeared at a public hearing to protest a proposed suburban rezoning which would have restricted conversions of large, old mansions. He charged that because most Negroes moved into apartments in converted single-family dwellings this was a poorly disguised effort to contain the Negro. A small proportion of the population excluded from the suburbs by snob zoning is Negro. A great majority of those being excluded cannot be really identified by race or religion. Their disqualification is measured only by the vague but binding rules of social stratification. Some communities such as the Detroit suburb, Grosse Pointe, have articulated these criteria of stratification to a fine degree, including a system which assigns varying numerical weights to varying ethnic backgrounds and has probably, by now, been programmed for a computer.[6]

But most communities are not so advanced in their techniques. The more general pattern involves the imposition of zoning and subdivision regulations so strict as to make development prohibitively expensive. These regulations are then varied downward only for those developers who the local leaders are confident will be properly selective in determining future residents. All of these techniques are justified by the superficially appealing slogan of protecting the local tax base.

There are lawyers who express apprehension over zoning's impact upon the American's traditional mobility. There are practitioners who remind us that the current practice of defending low density zoning on the ground that additional residents will increase the burden of public services conflicts with traditional and pioneer American convictions that the cost of services is irrelevant. Yet these attorneys are not unaware of the thicket into which such a line of reasoning leads. We have our established order of "constitutional rights" and it is not easy to find room for another statue in our pantheon. If labor has been unable to persuade society that a job is an inherent right, can one expect that such self-serving voices as the developer and such amorphous souls as the seeker after low-priced housing will persuade their fellow Americans that their interests supersede those of the local community?

Even the lawyer who is untroubled by lack of procedural or substantive due process encounters obstacles in zoning litigation which contribute to his frustrations in this field.

The first of these disabilities arises from the gulf in most zoning cases between the cost of presenting a good case and the value to the client of a successful result. The lawyer is frustrated to be restricted in the depth of his preparation by the scope of his client's investment. He knows that major landmarks in the law may be riding on the quality of his presentation. Yet, the immediate dispute may involve such parochial issues as the right of a suburb to eliminate a nonconforming billboard or junk yard, or the right of a community to prescribe the design of a single-family home. The decision, if it is of first impression in the state, will have an impact on all communities in the state and upon the present use of thousands of parcels of land. Zoning litigation is expensive and the clients are rarely large organizations; consequently an attorney is constantly forced either to decline litigation or to do a job his conscience considers less than adequate.

Zoning litigation is expensive because it is conducted almost exclusively through the use of expert testimony. The attorney must convey to the court a clear impression of the nature of the neighborhood with which the case is concerned. This generally requires the use of expertly prepared maps and photographs. Once this demonstrative evidence is in, the remainder of the case usually consists of expert testimony by planners, appraisers, traffic engineers, and other experts in the particular line of business involved in the case. Bona fide experts are expensive and even the phony ones cost something.

The expense of zoning litigation is compounded by the fact that the typical litigant is either a municipality operating on a very slim budget or is a private speculator whose willingness to pay legal fees is limited strictly by the profits he expects to make of the sale of the property. The inevitable result is that courts slide over important issues which are bypassed because of an inadequately presented case.

The kosher poultry dealer in the *Schlecter*[7] sick-chicken case gained his importance from the steel industry's determination to use this paltry vehicle as a weapon to defeat the NRA. There is no equivalent in the land-use field to the centralization of power and wealth which occurs in the income tax and labor fields and insures that many novel questions are thoroughly presented to the court even where the financial stake in the particular case may be small. It was Dick Cutler, a Milwaukee attorney, who made this point:

In income tax and labor matters counsel for each side usually represents so many clients having similar problems that he brings to even a small case a wealth of specialized knowledge. Unfortunately municipalities for various reasons do not encourage their counsel to develop the depth of specialization which will permit him in most cases to present to a court a sophisticated grasp of his field. The municipal lawyer is usually underpaid and given such a variety of general practice type of problems, such as liquor licenses, that he has little time budgeted for intensive research in the land-use planning field. Further, when even a fairly big land-use decision comes to his municipality, the city is seldom disposed to hire special counsel which might already be expert in the field.

The developer also has multiple reasons for presenting a weak challenge to the legal concepts being pursued, however inarticulately, by the municipality. Often he is afraid to challenge policies lest the city retaliate by denying him discretionary approval on some other project where his legal rights are small. Too, he frequently is a rugged individualist who will spend no more in fighting for a principle than the immediate profit which he stands to gain and seldom makes substantial contributions to a builder's organization where collective strength could bring the research and talent to bear which a major problem deserves.

I can recollect few cases since *Euclid* where this marshaling of equivalent adversary forces was apparent. The difference that can result when adequate evidence and skillful argument is presented to the court is illustrated in two 1963 cases involving trailers: a Pennsylvanian bought a trailer and sought a permit to build a permanent foundation under it and to use it as a single-family home on his two-acre lot. The township refused him permission because trailers were prohibited in residential zones. The Pennsylvania Mobilhome Association and the Mobil Home Dealers National Association joined in an appeal to the Pennsylvania Supreme Court. In an articulate and carefully reasoned opinion, that court held that the township's regulations discriminated against trailers and were therefore invalid. The decision, although one may disagree with it, will have a far-reaching effect in Pennsylvania and will be of immeasurable value to trailer manufacturers there and elsewhere.[8]

Within a few months of the time this case was decided in Harrisburg, the Illinois Supreme Court faced a very similar problem. A suburb of Chicago attempted to put out of business a small trailer camp operator. No trade association came to his assistance. The case was tried on the pleadings with no expert testimony. The operator's brief in the Illinois Supreme Court had only six pages of argument and cited only six cases, none of them remotely relevant. The court, in a short opinion which ignored the major issues raised by the case, ruled in effect that Illinois communities have virtually a free hand in dealing with trailer camps.[9]

If further evidence is needed of the intellectual sweetening that money can bring to zoning law, one need only look at the relatively few examples of cases in which large industry has become involved with zoning regulations. The most notable example in my state was when Knox County attempted to prohibit the strip mining of coal. The printed abstract of record that was presented to the Illinois Supreme Court was about a foot thick. A reading of the court's opinion is enough to show that counsel raised all of the major issues which could have been raised.[10]

Recently a small industry in Chicago challenged the industrial performance standards contained in the Chicago Zoning Ordinance. These are regulations which regulate not by permitting or prohibiting particular industrial uses but by setting standards for noise, odor, smoke, and other nuisance characteristics with which any industry must comply. A group of other industries, interested in supporting the regulations which would exclude nuisance type industries, retained Erwin Schulze, a Chicago attorney expert in industrial zoning regulations, to present their case. The result was an opinion of the Illinois Appellate Court soundly endorsing performance standard regulations which was, incidentally, the first opinion on industrial performance standards in the country.[11]

It has always seemed to me that many trade or professional associations would achieve more if the money they occasionally invest in drafting model codes or publishing exotic pamphlets were invested in *amicus* briefs in key zoning lawsuits. (Of course, my own professional bias may be showing here.)

This economic background goes a long way toward explaining the generally inadequate quality of most records and briefs in zoning cases. This is most striking in the cases which have been significant benchmarks. The *Saveland Park* v. *Wieland* decision in Wisconsin was, in my view, a crucial decision on the place of aesthetics in zoning law: the right of the community to control tastes in residential design.[12] Yet the record in this seminal case is almost casual in its brevity. This was a matter where the American Institute of Architects should have been involved up to their institutional gables—on one side or the other—to give the debate the depth it merited. Small wonder, though, that neither the attorney for the owner of a single lot nor the attorney for a small village could afford to marshal the expert testimony such an issue merited.

A Michigan attorney viewed the sad condition of zoning litigation this way:

> The difficulties are often that so many zoning cases are tried by city attorneys who are not trial lawyers and so much of the law that's made in this field is made by small-town city attorneys who may be good and competent men but who do not have access to a budget. They can't hire good experts. And they can't present a case. They don't have a lot of trial experience. All of these things. But those are the cases, bear in mind, which make the law. Now, that isn't true in the negligence field, you see. The more valuable the case you have in the negligence field, the more you can expend on expert witnesses. So what happens is this: that a judge can do what— Talbot Smith, [former justice of Michigan Supreme Court] a phrase he used, he said, 'The court is not required to close its eyes to that which is obvious to all mankind.' Well, in these zoning cases, I think many times the courts are confronted with a city attorney who has not put in a good case either through lack of funds or lack of interest—and many times it's lack of interest, bear in mind he's had a 4:3 split on his City Commission or maybe the complexion of the Commission has changed by this time. . . . You examine zoning case after zoning case and look into the briefs and records and you find that sometimes there isn't enough of a record to justify the opinion.

Another difficulty the lawyer must face—though the imaginative counsel may consider it an opportunity—are the great gaps in zoning law as made by the judges. If, as Justice Holmes observed, judges operate interstitially, they have a lot of sewing to finish in this field. The problem is not a lack of decisions but of decisions on basic techniques. When a community asks if it legally can do this or that, more frequently than not my reply has to be that the courts have not passed upon the issue. "I haven't the faintest idea what the courts will say but it is probable that the provision will remain unchallenged for ten years."

Many zoning techniques of dubious validity have gone unchallenged for years because they apply in situations which make it extremely difficult to challenge them. Perhaps the best example is architectural controls. Many cities have been applying architectural controls to single-family houses for forty years and have avoided a court test of their validity throughout this entire period. It is only rarely that the prospective builder of a single-family house has enough strength of architectural convictions that he is willing to incur the wrath of his neighbors and the time and expense of a long lawsuit rather than modify the design of the residence he proposes to build. Just recently an Ohio woman had enough conviction to challenge a decision of the Cleveland Heights Board of Architectural Review rejecting her proposal to build an atrium house among a covey of American Colonials. She carried the case to the appellate court, where the board's decision was upheld by two to one vote, but she then apparently decided that she could not afford to appeal the case to the Supreme Court of Ohio.[13]

Other types of zoning regulations are untested because they are used more often as nonlegal threats than as actual legal standards. The elimination of nonconforming uses without compensation is a good example. This technique is at least two decades old but the appellate decisions can be counted on your fingers. The primary reason for the lack of litigation is that municipalities are so dubious of the validity of this device that they hesitate to apply it if it will result in a substantial loss to the property owner. Consequently, amortization is typically applied only to signs and temporary structures where the property owner does not have sufficient investment involved to justify a legal challenge.

As a result, most routine zoning litigation is handled by lawyers who try and retry the same issues in the same pedestrian fashion.

"If a gasoline station is located on this corner, will it cause traffic congestion?" Or: "Is the traffic congestion already so heavy that it is unlawful to prohibit a gasoline station?" "Are the sizes of existing lots in the area large enough that it is fair to require new developers to build on 10,000 square feet?" Or: Is the "character of the surrounding area such that smaller lots should be permitted?" These arguments, framed in the language of the real estate appraiser, and ignoring everything that cannot be hit by a stone thrown from the property in question, have become the sole basis for the resolution of most zoning cases in this country.

Finally, the lawyer compounds his own perplexity in this field by his inability or unwillingness to understand the planner's value judgments. Frequently the lawyer insults the planner by his assumption that he is nothing more than an ethereal real estate appraiser who thinks in terms of "highest and best use" and whose judgment must be based upon the dollar consequence of alternative uses for the subject property. When the lawyer discovers that the planner's values are more universal than those of the real estate appraiser, confidence gives way to insecurity which, in the advocate, manifests itself through hostility.

It is true, as planners insist, that most lawyers do not understand planning. The more serious and accurate indictment is that this condition exists not because lawyers are stupid but because they do not want to understand planning. I have suggested in Chapter IV that planners, at least, are not easy to comprehend and planning itself is not easy to understand. But these obstacles do not excuse the practicing attorney's unwillingness to make the effort. I suspect in large part this is due to the lawyer's fear that planning involves meddling with the market. This results, of course, in the same ambivalence toward his profession that was noted among planners. The lawyer can resolve this ambivalence by rejecting planning; the planner, being American, cannot reject the market place.

The coolness of the lawyer toward urban planning is a tactical error, if nothing else. The advocate who intends to succeed in corporate law, negligence litigation or patent law comes to understand the premises and the argot of the accountant, physician, or engineer. To date, few lawyers have thought it necessary to establish a rapport with the planner. It is my hunch that in the next decade an intimate association with the lexicon, the myths, and the values of the planner is going to be imperative for more lawyers. Now that urban renewal has joined zoning and subdivision regulations as significant arenas for legal contests, the lawyer who has developed an empathy with those who practice these arts finds himself with more business than he can handle, while his brother who sneers at planners as wild-eyed dreamers may make noises on oral argument which sound good to his client—until the decree is entered.

The lawyer's unwillingness to engage in useful dialogue with the planner is not only a loss to the bar. It also penalizes the planner by denying him the experience of friendly challenge by the legal mind. If the bar became more intimate with the planning profession more lawyers would take the trouble to challenge some of the clichés and premises with which even the most sophisticated planners shield themselves. When we see the term "buffer" achieve the untouchable status it has when declaimed by planning witnesses in zoning litigation, and the word "compatibility" in a planning report assume a position where it is impertinent to question its meaning, the health of the profession requires a bloodletting. Other professions may regard lawyers as an insolent bunch of idol-smashers, but once the dialogue is established the accountants rethink their assumptions about the treatment of surplus and the physician reexamines his assumptions about the economic meaning of "disability." Likewise, until the bar turns its scorn or distaste for land use regulation into a positive concern for a resolution of the current three-way contest among private aspirations, municipal goals, and metropolitan needs, it is too much to ask that the planners do it alone.

The Judge

"This is another zoning case."
Supreme Court of Michigan,
Double I Development Co.
v. *Township of Taylor.*
125 N.W. 2d 862 (1964)

IF the observer is on rocky ground when he comments on the words and acts of other professionals, he is edging a precipice when he ventures opinions on the attitudes of the judiciary. My score before the bench being what it is, however, there are few falls that still hold any terror.

Throughout my travels I have interviewed many appellate and trial judges, and have obtained their comments and views on zoning law and zoning litigation. Their comments have been frank, blunt, and often incisive. Propriety prohibits me from identifying the informal comments of individual members of the bench. This chapter must consist, therefore, primarily of excerpts from formal written opinions plus anonymous quotes and paraphrases.

If the role of the lawyer has been inadequate, the posture of the bench toward zoning has been ambivalent and at times petulant. The courts, at least the appellate courts, genuinely dislike zoning litigation. I do not suggest that zoning stands alone in this judicial purgatory. Search and seizure cases, for example, undoubtedly present a similar resistance to rational jurisprudence. But zoning represents a new and significant portion of the appellate dockets and, unlike commercial or criminal law, there is an overtone of political and social consequence in each zoning case which only the most insensitive or secure bench can ignore. Even the judge who ordinarily enjoys his work usually finds the decision of zoning cases a very unrewarding form of labor. One appellate judge put it to me, "zoning is one of the most unsatisfactory areas of the law."

This judicial dislike for zoning can best be demonstrated by quoting from a few opinions. Justice Michael Mussmano of the Supreme Court of Pennsylvania expressed his distaste through a sort of wry humor:

> As a purse cannot be made from a sow's ear, so also a noisy, dust-laden restless community does not become a residential, tree-shaded quiet haven through the instrumentality of a zoning ordinance. A community is not like a petrified forest, indifferent to time, climate and world events. It is raw material in the hands of the invisible architect who shapes it according to the needs of the environment and the best interest of all the inhabitants in the area.[1]

Shades of social Darwinism! To demonstrate the comprehensiveness of the good judge's theological system, his "invisible architect" stoops to such lowly details as the design of aluminum awnings. This was proven when the township of Stonycreek tried to prevent Herman Heidorn and his wife Edna Mae from putting an aluminum awning and patio in front of their house in plain violation of the zoning ordinance. The township argued that if the Heidorns were allowed to prevail setback lines would become a nullity. Justice Mussmano responded:

> This is like worrying that the oceans will some day go dry. The law, while concerned about the future, focuses its attention on the immediate problem at hand and cannot allow an injustice to occur on the theory that a certain decision will become a ghost to haunt posterity. He cannot be influenced by the argument that if a certain privilege is allowed a hunchback, the whole world will become humpbacked.
>
> The short answer to the appellant's thesis in this field is that if our decision becomes a precedent to allow other exceptions to setback requirements, so let it be.[2]

Judge Mussmano's refusal to acknowledge a place for zoning in his invisible architecture is similar to the judicial "sit-in" conducted by the Supreme Court of Georgia. The Georgia court had held that zoning was invalid under the state's constitution. The voters then amended the constitution to permit zoning. When zoning again came before the Supreme Court, Chief Justice William Duckworth brushed off all of the court's earlier cases:

> A casual reading of the opinions in these cases reveals at once an absence of complete judicial comprehension of the problems at hand. This is easily understandable when it is recognized that lawyers and judges of this State before the dawn of constitutional consent to zoning of private property had become saturated with the fact that the Constitution respected and held inviolate private property. . . . But the people by their votes amended or changed this constitutional guardianship of private property, and in the process stripped their judiciary of power to protect it. . . . By the constitutional change the people voluntarily subjected their property to the unlimited control and regulation of legislative departments.[3]

The court ruled that it had no power to question the validity of any zoning regulation.

While few judges have expressed their irritation quite so colorfully as Mussmano or Duckworth about being forced to decide zoning cases, many appellate courts have discouraged zoning litigation in more orthodox fashion. Judge Mussmano, who seems to favor the landowner, has his opposite numbers in California, where the courts incline toward the municipality. "If reasonable minds may differ," says the California Supreme Court, "the ordinance will be sustained," and the court is very tolerant in its definition of a reasonable mind.

Thus in California it is possible to create a public beach by zoning property for use only as a "beach."[4] And in a recent case the supreme court saw no objection to zoning property for residential and agricultural uses although it was conceded that the property was virtually useless for any permitted purpose. In this latter case two justices of the United States Supreme Court voted to take the appeal, but the other seven were not interested.[5]

Some other courts have tried more formal methods to avoid zoning cases. On December 1, 1963, the following dispatch came over the Associated Press wires:

> PHILADELPHIA, Nov. 30 (AP).—Chief Justice John C. Bell said today the Pennsylvania Supreme Court no longer will hear zoning and other cases of little significance.
>
> The action is expected to cut the court's case load by 5 to 20 per cent.
>
> Justice Bell said the action is aimed primarily at appeals on rulings by zoning boards governing establishments such as neighboring beauty shops.[6]

The Illinois and New Jersey supreme courts have both interpreted new amendments to their respective state constitutions so as to channel almost all zoning cases to the intermediate appellate courts rather than to the Supreme Court.[7]

There is, in short, a pervading frustration on the part of the bench over the burgeoning role it must play in this area of the law. I sympathize with the judge who commented to me that "zoning is in a fog."

The roots of this judicial restlessness lie in the mess of local zoning administration. In those jurisdictions where the final local zoning decisions are "legislative," that is, are made by the city council, the courts are torn between their traditional reluctance to explore the motives of legislators and their suspicion that, as one appellate judge put it, "there's a lot of hanky-pank that we suspect but cannot find in the record."

It is apparent in many instances that the judge would prefer that these land-use matters came to him through administrative channels (such as the Board of Zoning Adjustment) rather than through the local legislature so that his inquiry would not be inhibited by the alleged separation-of-powers doctrine that purports to forbid judicial inquiry into legislative motives. One judge said:

> Now, I'm not too sure whether we shouldn't allow prudent motivational purposes to help us make up our minds on the borderline case. Theoretically we do not allow it whatsoever in Anglo-American

law right now; but in fact in many instances you find the judges working at it.

This lack of confidence in legislative responsibility, particularly when exercised by small political units, seems most evident in those judges who have come up through local politics. A state supreme court justice told me he decided at least one well-noted case against the municipality because he simply could not accept the view that officials of a small governmental unit were capable of exercising fairness where decisions on land-use matters required considerable discretion. A similar concern was put on the record by Illinios Supreme Court Justice Ray Klingbiel. He protested the majority's reasoning in a case involving the grant of a special use permit by a municipal legislative body:

> It is not part of the legislative function to grant permits, make special exceptions, or decide particular cases. Such activities are not legislative but administrative, quasi-judicial or judicial in character. To place them in the hands of legislative bodies, whose acts as such are not judicially reviewable, is to open the door completely to arbitrary government.[8]

In those jurisdictions where the local hearing is adminstrative, that is, before some board or appointed commission, and the courts can inquire more deeply into the local practice, the courts are shocked by the absence of those standards of procedure which they customarily expect from more dignified administrative agencies. "What, in truth," asked Justice Talbot Smith when he was on the Michigan Supreme Court, "was the warrant for the Board's action? We are not told. The Board says we do not have to be told."[9]

The Court of Appeals of Ohio expressed its impatience in this mild fashion, "It is unfortunate that the council of the municipality and the Board of Zoning Adjustment would allow such a situation to arise whereby there is no definite place to file the required papers,"[10] while a Texas appellate court declared "This [confused record] has necessitated a careful and tedious study of all of the testimony and in doing so our labor has been materially increased due to the very informal nature of the hearing before the Board."[11] In both the Ohio and Texas cases, the courts sustained the action of the municipality.

The incredible mishmash of local zoning procedure would be sufficient cause for judicial distaste for zoning cases. When, however, irresponsible administrative procedure is melded with intolerably dull factual records, the negative reaction of the bench is understandable. While academics, students, and devoted practitioners prefer to debate the merits of amortization of nonconforming uses, floating zones, industrial performance standards, density zoning, and similar challenging techniques, the view of zoning from the bench usually consists of a dispute over a proposal to put, say, a gas station on the corner of Third and Main. It is, indeed, dull business to have to commence an opinion with four pages of dreary recitation of all the land uses within a half mile of the subject property.

The factual brambles of most zoning cases and the corresponding absence of any clear and challenging legal issue are the primary reasons why most courts feel a sense of inadequacy when faced with writing a decision in a zoning case. "Gut instinct," is the way one appellate judge described his approach to zoning cases. The appellate courts should, indeed, have a sense of inadequacy in zoning cases. Most zoning cases, inherently parochial in their substantive issues and often irrelevant or incompetent in their administrative record, do not appear to call for detached judicial review as much as they require a super Board of Adjustment equipped with staff to probe the why of local decisions, and yet sufficiently detached from local pressure to provide the objectivity generally absent from local decision-making in land-use matters. Most appellate courts recognize that they are being used as an omnipotent Board of Adjustment and they know they are neither qualified nor equipped to perform the job.

Earlier it was emphasized that the old social and political labels of "conservative" and "liberal" are meaningless when we observe the layman's attitude toward zoning. The caveat applies with equal force to judicial attitudes. In the early days of zoning when courts were first struggling to extend the grasp of the police power to embrace this device, many of the cases of first impression involved efforts by communities to keep multiple-family dwellings out of single-family neighborhoods. The state courts upheld the technique but in most jurisdictions there were vehement protests from a minority of the justices. To me, the intriguing point about these protests was that these "conservative" judges, oriented toward the right of each property owner to deal in an unrestricted market, cloaked their objections not in words of concern for the inalienable property rights of the individual but in the economic and social consequences of classifying a community by housing type. It was the trial judge in the *Euclid* case, Judge Westenhaver, who noted that "in the last analysis, the result to be accomplished is to classify the population and segregate them according to their income or situation in life."[12] It is not apparent that Judge Westenhaver and justices of state supreme courts in the 1920's who made equally ineffective protests were generally motivated by a Brandeisian egalitarianism. Yet when it came to zoning, their articulated reasons, at least, had such a timbre.

Today the same peculiar inversion is apparent in the attitudes of those judges who are inclined in zoning litigation to give a substantial benefit of doubt to the municipality. These socially oriented arbiters talk about the "presumption of validity" of the act of a local legislature which represents one five-hundredth of the population of a metropolitan area. This is the same judge whose belief in a passive role for the bench in reviewing social legislation arises out of his belief in the righteousness of that legislation. Yet he is not aware that the social consequences of extending the same presumption of validity to the land-use decisions of a single municipal corporation will frequently produce results that are in direct conflict with the premises which motivate him when he reviews social legislation at the state or national level. It is frequently charged and often apparent, that local zoning practices on the fringes of metropolitan areas are designed to keep out the distasteful aspects of urbanization while permitting access to its fruits. These practices create exclusionary conditions directly in conflict with goals of social mobility and economic opportunity. The "liberal" judge endorses state or federal legislation designed to further these goals and he endorses local legislation which frustrate these policies.

One midwestern justice put it bluntly: "As long as the communities don't impinge on race or religion I say let them do as they please." Few judges have yet sensed this contradiction in their attitudes. Justice Frederick Hall of New Jersey, in his remarkable dissent in *Vickers* v. *Gloucester Township* is a voice crying in the wilderness:

> The majority decides that this particular municipality may constitutionally say, through exercise of the zoning power, that its residents may not live in trailers—or in mobile homes, to use a more descriptive term. I am convinced such a conclusion in this case is manifestly wrong. Of even greater concern is the judicial process by which it is reached and the breadth of the rationale. The import of the holding gives almost boundless freedom to developing municipalities to erect exclusionary walls on their boundaries, according to local whim or selfish desire, and to use the zoning power for aims beyond its legitimate purposes. Prohibition of mobile home parks, although an important issue in itself, becomes, in this larger aspect, somewhat a symbol.[13]

Until the "liberal" bench sees these issues as frequently involving something more than just landowner versus village they are not likely to be moved by pleas that local land-use decisions must accommodate themselves to metropolitan or regional needs and aspirations. Were this transformation to occur the property-oriented "conservative" judge and the socially-oriented "liberal" judge would find themselves jointly condemning local land-use practices for totally divergent, if not incompatible, reasons. This dialogue took place with attorney David Craig, in Pittsburgh:

> BABCOCK: Do you think the minority view which tends to be conservative or skeptical about local land-use powers reflects simply a property orientation? Or does it reflect the sort of view that's expressed by Hall in his dissent in *Vickers*—a suspicion that behind

some of these regulations are not anti-property bias but exclusionary techniques?

CRAIG: The whole expression of this conservative view in Pennsylvania has been in terms of property—property rights—entirely. The concern about exclusion within a region and exclusionary barriers within a region has not been voiced at all in the Pennsylvania decisions.

BABCOCK: Do you believe it is conceivable that perhaps some of the so-called liberal judges might find themselves eventually on the same side as the conservative judges—for different reasons?

CRAIG: Yes. In fact, I could easily visualize this coming about if the so-called liberal judges, who are concerned in a sense more about the comprehensive plan than about property rights, should become enamored of a regional plan. Then, it seems to me, their loyalty to the comprehensive plan for the region might cause them to be concerned about exclusionary aspects of individual municipality's regulations within the region. But I doubt if they would then frame their opposition to those restrictions in terms of general welfare. I suspect they would frame it again in terms of inconsistency with a pattern.

At the start of this commentary on the bench I warned that the difficulties of generalization are substantial. In large part this is because much of what takes place at the local level never gets into court. Generalizing is dangerous also because each state supreme court, depending upon the degree of urbanization in the jurisdiction, has demonstrated different attitudes toward municipal efforts to impede or circumvent the consequences of metropolization. Within the context of land-use disputes, the scope of the police power and substantive due process takes in the entire spectrum of judicial attitude. Compare, for example, the attitudes of the Minnesota Supreme Court or the Appellate Courts of Ohio with the opinions of the highest courts in California and Connecticut. The persistence of this variegated condition is largely attributable to the reluctance of the United States Supreme Court to grant certiorari in zoning cases. Shortly after *Euclid* the Court took on *Nectow* v. *City of Cambridge*[14] and established the right of the bench to review particular applications of the general technique sanctioned in *Euclid*. Since that time the United States Supreme Court has stoutly resisted attempts to foist on it responsibility in this area. I would like to believe that among the justices of our highest court, conservative or liberal, Democrat or Republican, southerner or Yankee, corporate lawyer or ex-professor, there has been consensus on only one point: if we cherish our equilibrium, never agree to review a zoning case.

Forty-nine out of fifty zoning cases have no business crowding the dockets of state supreme courts, yet that one should be decided only by the highest court in the state. When the Illinois Supreme Court, after thirty years of deciding zoning cases, finally decided to forego that dubious pleasure it still appeared to reserve to itself the responsibility to review some zoning cases:

> Of course there will be zoning cases that question the validity of particular provisions of the enabling statute, or that involve the use of new and unfamiliar techniques. A case of this type, that presents novel and substantial constitutional issues of concern to every community in the State, will sustain a direct appeal to this court.[15]

199 out of 200 zoning cases have no call upon the Supreme Court of the United States. Yet that one case will raise an issue of sufficient universality and dignity to make divergent rules among the states intolerable. Amortization of nonconforming uses without compensation, the right totally to exclude non-nuisance uses from a community, and the power to impose minimum size on houses; these are a few examples of practices which should have a common rule throughout the fifty states. In the context of economic and social interdependency within which our municipalities find themselves, it makes no sense to view zoning as no more than a form of private and local real estate law, or, worse, as the exclusive franchise of each municipal duchy. Zoning must be treated as a matter of public policy which has metropolitan implications. And as we pass from the intra-state metropolis to the age of Jean Gottman's Megalopolis this fact becomes more obvious. In the sensitive area of land-use policy Chicago is not separable from its suburbs, and those satellites spill into Wisconsin and Indiana. Indeed, to avoid

real discrimination and distortion in the application of municipal land-use policy, substantial uniformity of policy and administration by New York, New Jersey, and Connecticut and by Pennsylvania, Delaware, and New Jersey is called for.

What is required from all the participants, laymen, planners, lawyers, and judges is an effort to turn zoning from the petty, parochial device it now is to a viable tool of land-use policy.

Part 2

The Rules

The Purpose of Zoning

7~8

> "In the perfect market, natural zoning would result."
>
> Ratcliff

> "The witness, I have inferred, takes the position that good zoning requires that this property-holder . . . should be protected against himself."
>
> Record on Appeal. *Corthouts*
> v. *Town of Newington,*
> 140 Conn. 284 (1953)

THE most fun as well as the safest path for the amateur commentator is to keep things anecdotal. But even the practicing attorney, faced with the duty to discharge immediate assignments, is not free from the impulse to point the way. Hence my intention in this and the following chapters to consider a few of the issues underlying most disputes involving public regulation of private land.

Why do we have zoning anyway?

It is indicative of the chaotic nature of the subject that there is no generally accepted answer to this question. At the start I suggested that zoning caught on as an effective technique to further an eminently conservative purpose: the protection of the single-family house neighborhood. In spite of all the subsequent embellishments that objective remains paramount. As might be expected, such a motive is rarely articulated as a rationale for this popular device, either by the supporters or critics of zoning.

115

There are, however, some plausible theories offered in support of zoning. I am not concerned here with the deeper psychological motivations which drive many of the backers of zoning. These may vary from a fear of Negro infiltration to a vague identification of zoning with "good government." While they cannot be ignored by anyone practicing in this field, I am concerned here with more rational purposes of zoning.

We can dismiss the early legal fictions which were created to validate zoning under the jurisprudence of the 1920's. The early proponents of zoning claimed that the single-family district was insulated to prevent the spread of fires. Minimum house size requirements were supposedly related to public health. Billboards were said to endanger public morals because of the promiscuous activities which took place behind them. No one really believed these fictions in 1920 and no one believes them today. And today our courts have progressed beyond the need for this type of shibboleth.

I have found in circulation two relatively rational theories of the purpose of zoning which I refer to as the "property value" theory and the "planning" theory. For the purpose of clarifying the issues let me state these theories in a generalized fashion.

THE PROPERTY VALUE THEORY

To most real estate brokers and promoters, and to some land economists, lawyers, and judges, zoning is a means of maximizing the value of property. The use of property, under this theory, is basically determined by the dynamics of the market. Denver attorney George Creamer speaks for this view:

> The dynamics of a community, so long as that community remains economically free, dictate the uses to which land will inevitably gravitate, whatever expedient of zoning be employed. Zoning otherwise employed than as a braking mechanism is probably misapplied, and, historically, is probably futile.[1]

Although the exponents of this theory purport to believe in the dominance of free market forces, they are strong supporters of zoning. This paradox can be understood only by the realization that under this theory the "proper" zoning of property is determined by market forces. Zoning is merely an adjunct to the market mechanism.

The basic axiom of this theory is that each piece of property should be used in the manner that will insure that the sum of all pieces of property will have maximum value, as determined by market forces. In other words, every piece of property should be used in the manner that will give it the greatest value (i.e., its "highest and best use") without causing a corresponding decrease in the value of other property. The zoning ordinance can achieve this goal by prohibiting the construction of "nuisances," provided the common-law concept of nuisance is extended to include any use which detracts from the value of other property to a degree significantly greater than it adds to the value of the property on which it is located.

In the Property Value theory, for every piece of land there is a "proper" zoning classification. Above every town there exists a Platonic ideal zoning map, waiting to be dropped into place. This map shows for each piece of property the use or uses which will give to the sum of all property the greatest total value. This theory is what enables many judges to determine the proper zoning classification for property based solely on the estimates of appraisers of the value of the property and surrounding property under various zoning classifications. The Property Value theory requires only ordinary arithmetic, and has the appeal of all simple solutions to complex problems.

A corollary of the Property Value theory is that the planners tend to be meddlers who, by their tinkering, upset the natural market forces. Zoning, properly concerned, does no more than protect the market from "imperfections" in the natural operation of supply and demand. Professor Richard Ratcliff, economist at the University of Wisconsin, is an outspoken proponent of this view:

> We start with the premise that the arrangement of community land uses should be the product of social preferences; and that, but for

the imperfections of the real estate market, the market interactions of demand and supply would create a city so organized. Thus we view city planning as a device for releasing the basic forces of demand rather than inhibiting them.[2]

If Professor Ratcliff's outlook had too much the appearance of economic determanism, it remained for Allison Dunham, University of Chicago law professor, to soften Ratcliff's dictum and to provide a rationale by which all local control over private development could be justified: public control in all events is justified, but in some cases there must be compensation to the landowner.

Dunham, the lawyer, sensed the social flaw in economist Ratcliff's theory. "With respect to private land use decisions," he said, "considerations of economy and efficiency are reflected in the market price, but no beneficial or detrimental impact of a land use upon other lands is reflected in the market for a particular land use."[3] The public may take (regulate) says Dunham but "[t]he public need not compensate an owner when it takes (restricts) his privileges of ownership in order to prevent him from imposing a cost upon others; but when the state takes (uses or restricts) his property rights in order to obtain a public benefit it must compensate him."

As for the role of the planner, Dunham decrees: "The city planner may interfere with and supervise the land use decisions of a private developer only because of the interaction of one land use upon another and only then where the private developer's land use adversely affects others."

I am not sure I understand what he means by "interaction" but I suspect Professor Dunham is saying that any control by a municipality over private land use is justified by that municipality's goals, but that development cannot be forbidden or regulated without compensation unless it has a direct and demonstrably adverse impact on neighboring land. The community may without compensation stop X from developing a subdivision of half-acre lots if the consequence would be overflowing septic tanks ("a cost upon others"); but the community cannot, without compensation, re-

quire Y to build only on three-acre lots if three-acre lots are required not for reasons of public health but simply because a
majority happen to prefer that kind of living.

There are two difficulties with this market-oriented theory, even
with Dunham's cash sweetener.

( ) In the first place, under this theory any land use which unduly
lowers the value of neighboring property has to be a "nuisance."
Whether the municipality, in order to regulate, should pay or need
not pay depends on the degree of adverse impact. But the blind
concentration on property values can hide less savory values that
may not be entitled to protection, whether by uncompensated regulation or by cash payment. The Property Value theory does not
ask why a particular development has an adverse impact on values
of neighboring property.

New Jersey lawyer-planner Norman Williams illustrates:

> When the argument is made that property values will be affected
> what is meant is simply that some factor is present which some
> people may dislike, and which may therefore tend to result in a
> net reduction in the number of people interested in buying property
> in the area affected—thus tending to push values down. The real
> question is always a simple one—what is the factor which is in-
> volved? Some factors which affect property values (or which are
> thought to do so) are legitimate subjects for public regulation, by
> zoning or otherwise; others are not. For example, the invasion of
> factories and the movement of Negroes into a residential neighbor-
> hood both may be thought to affect property values. Yet one is
> obviously a proper subject for zoning protection, while the other
> is not. The fact that property values may be affected gives reason
> to look into the situation, but by itself tells nothing about whether
> governmental protection is appropriate.[4]

To use zoning as a tool solely for protecting the values of neighboring property is an extreme form of parochialism our society
cannot afford in the twentieth century. As Finley Peter Dunne
pointed out, it is possible to cheer too loudly for the rights of
property:

> But I'm with th' rights iv property, d'ye mind. Th' sacred rights an'

th' divine rights. A man is lucky to have five dollars; if it is ten, it is his dooty to keep it if he can; if it's a hundred, his right to it is th' right iv silf-dayfinse; if it's a millyon, it's a sacred right; if it's twinty millyon, it's a divine right; if it's more thin that, it becomes ridickilous. In anny case, it mus' be proticted. Nobody mus' intherfere with it or down comes th' constichoochion, th' army, a letther fr'm Baer an' th' wrath iv Hivin.[5]

I am disturbed for another reason by the Ratcliff-Dunham apology for zoning. Both spokesmen do not define the scope of the "public" whose interest justifies some public limitation on the free market forces. There appears in their thinking a view that private development can be limited by regulation (or compensation) only where there is a direct and adverse impact upon a neighbor's land, or upon the municipality in which the land happens to be located. Both views assume a parochial definition of the "public" that will be affected by land development. Ratcliff sees the "imperfections of the real estate market" as equivalent to essentially local forces and Dunham obviously is concerned with impact upon land uses in the immediate neighborhood. In the former case, I suspect the emphasis is explained by a lack of interest in regional consequences of local land-use development; the Dunham amendment suggests not indifference but a firm rejection of the idea that metropolitan or regional interests have any place in the municipal regulation or, indeed, the taking of private land.

I believe that in many cases the reasonableness of zoning should be determined by reference to factors far more complex than a simple balancing of values of neighboring property, whether or not cash boot is tossed on to the scales. This doubt leads to my disenchantment with the other doctrinal justification for zoning.

THE PLANNING THEORY

I suppose that every city planning student is required to write on the blackboard a hundred times the Planner's Oath: "Zoning is merely a tool of planning." Walter Blucher asked some years ago if the zoning tail was wagging the planning dog. The question points up the view of the planner that zoning is only a minor appendage to the essential body, city planning.

Standard planning dogma requires that a planner invited to prepare a municipal zoning ordinance go through the following ritual: First, a very junior planner makes a survey of the municipality and prepares a map showing the land uses. On the basis of this and reams of other data, and of consultations with community leaders, a very senior planner prepares a "comprehensive plan" for the community, which indicates the community's idea of what it wishes its future to be. The planner then sets forth a number of means for "implementing" the plan, including, typically, a capital improvements program, a subdivision control law, and a zoning ordinance. In the planner's view, understandably, the zoning ordinance is merely one of a number of methods of effectuating an overall municipal plan.

I do not suggest that this exercise should be abandoned. It is a laudable if not legally essential exercise for a community to analyze and articulate its communal goals and objectives before it enacts controls over the use of private land. This discipline, required by law if not in fact in England, has not achieved the responsible status it should have in this country. This is Harvard Professor Haar's "impermanent constitution," the comprehensive municipal plan. It is said that only when the community has, in its plan, set forth and exposed to public scrutiny its goals and desires can the arbiter, required to settle land use disputes, measure the reasonableness of the implementing ordinances. Professor Haar explains:

> To the professional planner, the dependence of zoning upon planning is relatively simple and clear. The city master plan is a long-term general outline of projected development; zoning is but one of the many tools which may be used to implement the plan. Warnings have constantly emanated from the planners that the two must not be confused. . . .
>
> The legal implications of this theory seem manifest. A city undertaking to exercise the land regulatory powers granted to it by state enabling legislation should be required initially to formulate a master plan, upon which regulatory ordinances, of which the zoning ordi-

nance is but one, would then be based. Such ordinances could be judicially tested not only by constitutional standards of due process and equal protection, but also by their fidelity to the specific criteria of the master plan.[6]

Thereby is born the "principle" that a zoning ordinance must (should) be based upon a plan.

What, then, is a Plan? Hugh Pomeroy defined it this way:

> Well—what do we mean by comprehensive plan? The nearest I can come to defining it is this: it is a plan that makes provision for all the uses that the legislative body of that municipality decides are appropriate for location somewhere in that municipality. That's Number 1. Number 2, it makes provision for them at the intensities of use that the legislative body deems to be appropriate. In Number 3—the locations that the legislative body deems to be appropriate. That is the mechanical concept. Beyond that the plan should consistently represent developmental objectives for the community. And if you can have a good enough statement of developmental objectives, then I don't think that a deviation from a particular mechanical device such as regulations by districts—the departure from that—violates the attribute of comprehensiveness that consists in endeavoring to carry out these objectives.

Perhaps what troubles me about this definition is not what it says but what it implies. The corollary to this precept, accepted by many lawyers (though not Professor Haar), and by most planners and laymen is that the validity of local land-use laws should be measured *only* by their consistency with the municipal plan. This is no more of a valid purpose for zoning than is the concept of the use district. The public disclosure of municipal objectives may be a necessary first step by which equal treatment of similarly situated individuals within the municipality can be determined. To this extent the municipal plan serves as a useful intramural yardstick for the municipal regulations. The local plan in this sense is imperative as a device to bring some consistency and impartiality in local administrative decisions among residents of the same municipality.

It is an error, however, to dignify the municipal plan with more authority than this limited function. But to measure the validity of zoning by the degree to which it is consistent with a municipal plan does just that. The municipal plan may be just as arbitrary and irresponsible as the municipal zoning ordinance if that plan reflects no more than the municipality's arbitrary desires. If the plan ignores the responsibility of the municipality to its municipal neighbors and to landowners and taxpayers who happen to reside outside the municipal boundaries, and if that irresponsibility results in added burdens to other public agencies and to outsiders, whether residents or landowners, then a zoning ordinance bottomed on such a plan should be as vulnerable to attack as a zoning ordinance based upon no municipal plan.

The trouble, then, with the Planning Theory of zoning is that by deifying the municipal plan it enshrines the municipality at a moment in our history when every social and economic consideration demands that past emphasis on the municipality as the repository of the "general welfare" be rejected. More about this in Chapter IX.

It has to be conceded, however, that zoning has been a huge success in most of our suburbs if the Planning Theory of zoning means doing with land what the municipality alone wants done, provided it announces its intentions in advance. If planning is designed to provide that environment which a majority of the voters within the boundaries of a particular municipality believe they want, then zoning has been remarkably successful and I predict it will prosper. Indeed, if planning is intended to achieve not only physical amenities but also to accomplish some unstated or whispered social and political objectives, zoning has been far more effective than its originators dared expect. In this sense, far from being a "negative tool" zoning has been a positive force shaping the character of the municipality to fits its frequently vague but nevertheless powerful preconceptions.

If, when we speak of planning, we postulate objective standards for physical environment and let the social chips fall where they may, then zoning as an implement of planning has not merely failed but has been instrumental in the failure of planning. This failure is pernicious. Like another Noble Experiment with about the same birthdate as zoning, it erodes the civic conscience by permitting us to wrap our selfish anti-democratic aims in a garment of public interest.

I suppose what really disturbs me is that because zoning is the most universal of all the legal tools for shaping the character of the municipality, any unwise use of the process has a far greater impact upon our national character than does the abuse of a less widely employed device for control of land use. The zoning power is so fragmented that its abuse does not have a dramatic impact. Dollar venality in the execution of one urban redevelopment project will receive strident and outraged attention from the metropolitan press, while daily evidence of intellectual dishonesty and moral corruption in the application of zoning in our suburban areas is accepted as a civic norm. If you are of the school which has as its premise that each of the hundreds of municipal units in a politically fragmented system of local government may regulate as it pleases and exclude whom and what it chooses to exclude, then you should embrace the present state of affairs and the existence of a municipal plan is sufficient. If, however, you suspect, as I do, that the current practice impinges not merely upon property rights but upon some less tangible values which are important in a democratic society, then it is time to redefine our goals and to restate the Planning Theory of zoning in the hope that this exercise may lead us to reshape our implements for land-use control.

In my opinion there can never be any single foreordained purpose of zoning. Both the Planning Theory and the Property Value Theory of zoning set forth valid goals for some people in some situations. Their proponents err only when they set up their hypothesis as the one valid purpose of zoning. They err when they try to turn zoning into a tool to implement only their own local purposes.

Zoning needs no purposes of its own. Zoning is no longer a "movement" like the Single Tax or Prohibition; zoning is a process.

It is that part of the political technique through which the use of private land is regulated. When zoning is thought of as a part of the governmental process it is obvious that it can have no inherent principles separate from the goals which each person chooses to ascribe to the political process as a whole.

While we should not insist that zoning have "purposes" we can insist that the zoning process be exercised in accord with certain principles, that the "means" if not the "ends" of zoning be governed by neutral principles. This necessitates an inquiry into (a) whether zoning has spawned its own indigenous set of principles, or whether it is subject merely to the principles applicable to other forms of governmental action; and (b) whether it makes sense to restrict the zoning debate to only two parties: the landowner and the local municipality.

VIII

The Principles of Zoning

> "Folks all know what planning principles are."
> Corwin Mocine, Professor of Planning,
> University of California

WEBSTER defines "principle" as "a comprehensive and fundamental law, doctrine, or assumption." This is an acceptable definition if we assume that the words carry with them by implication the phrase "with a continuing validity."

By this definition there are no principles unique to zoning. Some planners to the contrary notwithstanding, the only meaningful principles applicable to land-use planning in a democratic society are equally germane to other areas of human endeavor. Much of the confusion in land-use regulation stems from our repeated inclination to canonize short-range devices and techniques. One of the major obstacles to a sensible analysis of zoning policy and practice has been the failure of most commentators and judges to distinguish between principles, on the one hand, and techniques, on the other. The former should be continuing and capable of universal application. The latter should be continuously reexamined in the light of changes in social needs and in technology. Unfortunately too many zoning techniques have been elevated to the status of principles.

The most notorious example of this confusion is the use district.

The birthmark of zoning was the division of the community into zones or districts, each with designated use, bulk, and open space regulations. Clearly implied was the injunction that there be a district for each use. Not all commentators have gone as far as did the Supreme Court of New Jersey when it condemned the classification of all land in a township into a single zone as "alien to the constitutional and statutory principle of land use zoning by districts."[1] Nevertheless, in spite of the current skepticism about zoning, we still tend to be mesmerized by the use district "principle." We forget that the use district was an ingenious device placed in our statutes to overcome what was believed to be a legal obstacle; namely, the need to overcome the legal infirmities of the old block ordinances by providing a comprehensive scheme of regulation for the entire municipality. The use district is not an immutable yardstick by which the validity of regulations over land use must be measured. Districting is nothing more than a legislative device that should not be insulated from scrutiny and should be discarded if it is no longer viable. We are in the process of doing just that through our *ad hoc* contrivances to grant special dispensations from the rigidity of districting. The trouble is that these improvisations are combined with a pretense of districting, apparently because we fear to challenge overtly the "principle" of districting.

Nothing better illustrates the unprincipled status of the "district" concept than a review of the way we have employed it during the last forty years.

From 1920 to 1940 districting was "cumulative." That is, if a community had four districts—single-family, multiple-family, business, and industrial—the first was the "highest," the last was the "lowest." All the uses permitted in the "highest" single-family district were also permitted the other three districts. Uses permitted in the "second," multiple-family district, were also permitted in the business and industrial zones until the industrial zone became the garbage pail for all uses, including residences. This "pour-over" dogma apparently was based on what seemed to be a logical application of the Property Value theory of zoning. Proximity of a residential zone to a railroad yard, so the theory ran, argues for using the property for housing poorer families at higher densities because that would increase overall property values. The nuisance concept was also reflected in the common practice in early ordinances that simply designated heavy industrial areas in an "Unclassified Zone." The owner of land in that zone was no worse off than before zoning. Being a nuisance or potential nuisance himself, there was nothing from which he needed protection. And the misguided or unfortunate person whose home was located in a lower zone had only himself to blame. During the springtime of zoning, this cumulative doctrine was an indisputable "principle" to the courts, the layman, the planner, and the local legislator.

After World War II, there became popular the planning "principle" that each district should be exclusively reserved for the uses deemed appropriate in that district. If it was bad public policy to interlard residences with business and industry in residential districts it was equally unsound to permit such an intermixture elsewhere. No longer was there a hierarchy of uses. Each class of uses had an equal dignity and each was entitled to protection from the baleful results of exposure to the other. If the industrial pigs were to be kept out of the residential parlor, then those who enjoyed the parlor should most certainly stay out of the pen. The "separate but equal facilities" doctrine came to zoning. This repudiation of the old ways was not accomplished without some pulling and hauling in the courts and it did create difficult political if not legal problems: an exclusive industrial district meant that single-family residences in that district became nonconforming uses, and we hesitated to apply the same limitations to their expansion as we applied to nonconforming business and industrial uses in residential zones.

This new approach also reflected the increased sophistication and self-confidence of the professional planner. He was convinced that it was not only proper but feasible to predict the best direction and type of growth in each community. The "master plan" for future municipal growth could be put on a map, thereby designating the appropriate use of each section of the community in advance of development. This premise led to the marking of uncumulative, exclusive districts on the zoning map, even outside the developed areas. (Note that the widespread use of this technique meant quite a victory of the Planning Theory of zoning over the Property Value theory that had initially made zoning so successful. The predetermined visual plan was in the ascendancy and "exclusive" districting was a logical method of implementing this rigid concept.)

Given the system of zoning as practiced in most communities, there was much that made sense in the new "principle" of exclusive districting. The indiscriminate push of residential uses into commercial zones undermined the cohesiveness of the business area and increased the pressure for strip commercial zoning. As long as a landowner could build either residences or stores in the Commercial District he was bound to prefer commercial zoning. If he were limited solely to commercial development in the Commercial District he might, it was hoped, weigh his prospects more critically.

Undoubtedly the general acceptance of this new "principle" was aided by the thrust of industry to the suburbs and the consequent desire to guard potential industrial sites from fragmentation by nonindustrial development. The general enthusiasm with which local chambers of commerce endorsed the reservation of industrial areas for industrial uses suggested there was merit in the claim that industrial development was retarded or diverted by the delays and costs of clearing title to tracts which had been abortively subdivided for residential purposes even though zoned for industrial use. Industry could operate with greater freedom if it knew it would not have to contend with homeowners as neighbors. Exclusive districting had many attractions to the suburbs, not the least of which was the possibility of diverting "undesirable" residential growth by zoning large tracts exclusively for industrial use. No one pretended there was an industrial potential comparable to the acreage so zoned, but the New Jersey exurb (caught between the population pressure south from Newark and the thrust north from Trenton) that zoned half its territory for exclusive industrial purposes could not be accused of the heresy of creating a single residential zone for the entire municipality.

The unstated consequence of the "principle" of exclusive districts, however, was that it underscored the differences between uses and discouraged a search for a way to recognize and express in the law the similarities between different uses. This result was bound to cause trouble in an era of increasing social mobility and massive changes in building technology and design.

Professor Corwin Mocine, of the University of California, Berkeley, noted the dangers in making a firm principle of the exclusive district concept:

> One of the things that seems to me very serious is the idea of several one-class districts—one-use districts—which has traditionally been part of zoning, has been so deeply imbedded in public consciousness that now, when we've found that perhaps something else is more desirable, we can't accomplish it because people feel that somehow or other this is improper and that you're violating good planning principles.

The principle of exclusive districts had barely been established by the early fifties when some rebels began to challenge it. These iconoclasts proposed mixing the uses. Reminiscent of the jazz singer, they took up the refrain: "It's not whatcha do, it's the way thatcha do it." There is now a growing and articulate band who insist that there is nothing sacred about the "principle" of use segregation. They propose that we identify the offensive characteristics rather than ban the use.

This current restlessness with segregating the uses reflects, in part, a growing disenchantment with the validity of the visual or mapped master plan. No longer do all planners believe that it is both necessary and possible that the law forecast the precise direction and kind of growth. The increasing substitution of verbal plans—statements of municipal objectives—for mapped or graphic master plans reflects an awareness that precision in prediction is not feasible, and classification by use is not so simple a guide to sensible urban development.

The attack upon exclusive districts did not start with a frontal assault upon the single-family district but with the seduction of that less reputable gal, the industrial area. Like all shrewd innovators, the protagonists of the new idea came up with a slogan: "performance standards." Why, indeed, should the classification of industrial districts into light, medium, and heavy be based upon what was produced in a factory? Why cling to the rubric of the Heavy Industrial District use list—abattoir to yeast plant—if a meat packer with a deft sense of public relations or an unfortunate allergy decided to minimize the odors commonly associated with his industry? Let him operate in the Light Industrial District if he could meet the standards of that zone.

In a few years the legal barriers between different industrial uses have been cracked if not demolished by the technique of "industrial performance standards." Under this concept, if a community has three industrial districts, Light, Medium, and Heavy, the permissible location of a particular plant depends upon the nuisance characteristics of the plant irrespective of what it produces. The test is based upon the noise, odor, smoke, vibration, and fire hazard generated by that particular plant. Precise formulae for these characteristics are set out in the ordinance, the standards in the Heavy Industrial District being less stringent than the corresponding standards in the Light Industrial District. Conceivably one paint factory might have to locate in the Heavy District while a competitor who was willing to invest in odor and smoke controls could locate in the Light Industrial District. The idea has been so infectious that even the village which can barely process an application for a permit to build a single-family bungalow on a forty-foot lot now has a zoning ordinance peppered with phrases such as "Ringleman Chart," "Octave Band" and "Odor Threshold." Norman Williams observed: "It is a bit fantastic to make a big deal about working out more elaborate planning controls involving much more complex administration, and then to turn them over to administrative machinery which can't keep track of a copy of the current zoning map."[2]

If performance standards make sense in industrial zones, why not apply them across the board? (One response is that to do so would outlaw many of the "amenities" we enjoy in our residential zones! In one instance my associate, Fred Bosselman, proposed that a Chicago suburb apply the performance standards for noise and smoke of the Light Industrial District to the Single-Family District. He was advised by engineers that nearly all window air conditioners and power mowers in the residential neighborhoods would not conform and that the emission from a number of house chimneys would be illegal.)

There is no logical reason why the intermixing that is now acceptable in the case of industry should not be equally valid in other districts. Intermixing of dwelling types, of apartments and duplexes and single-family uses based upon non-use standards, is just as rational as the intermixing of a varnish factory with a plastics plant. The concept of "vertical zoning" reflected in the stratification of apartments and shops in one building requires the use of nuisance techniques similar in concept to those employed in industrial performance standards. The hitch, of course, is that we have one set of mores for the industrial pigs and another for the residential parlors. The introduction of multiple-family uses into a single-family zone carries social implications which are absent in the treatment of industry.

There is nevertheless evidence that even the residential districts are not immune to the "performance standard" technique. This susceptibility is apparent in the current popularity of the so-called Planned Unit Development. This is the antithesis of the exclusive districting "principle."

This clamor for greater flexibility has one persuasive argument going against it. While the advocates of these new approaches label the districting concept as rigid, the supporters of the rigid district concept insist that the more appropriate characterization is certainty. At least under districting the landowner knows in advance what he can and cannot do, and the co-called rigidity inherent in districting carries with it an ease of administration that permits the smallest village to handle zoning with greater speed and certainty. Conventional regulations may be either over-strict or over-permissive but this is a lesser evil than the vagueness inherent in the repudiation of use districts.

The significant fact is that industrial performance standards and, less certainly, planned developments, are a crack in the door, the thin edge of the wedge as the British call it. The "principle" of exclusive use districts has been violated with impunity. And we are almost full circle to our original thesis of cumulative or pour-over zoning but with the difference that the technique works both ways: up and down, if you please, for the Colonel's (residential) lady, as well as for Susie (non-residential) O'Grady.

In the light of this ambivalent history it is impertinent to treat the technique of districting as a fundamental doctrine or assumption with continuing validity. Districting is no more a principle than a statutory 35 mph speed zone is a principle. It is a legislative technique whose integrity should not be an untouchable premise but an assumption subject to continuous challenge and to proof of its present validity. This is not to suggest that the use district should be abandoned; only that it should be recognized as a technique to be used only where appropriate, and not a universal principle.

What benchmark is left then for those of us who are concerned with zoning? If there are no principles—only techniques—to serve as guides for decision-making in the regulation of land use, where is the pole star?

The heart of the matter is that the principles in this area of human activity, zoning, are no different from those fundamental assumptions which guide us in other areas of human intercourse. In our society they are constitutional and they are invoked by phrases such as equal protection and procedural due process, by the debate over the scope of "general" in the phrase "general welfare," and by the continuing dialogue over the appropriate boundaries of the police power and the power of eminent domain.

Perhaps I can illustrate the application of these principles in land-use law.

I noted earlier that a comprehensive municipal land-use plan can serve as a useful yardstick for measuring the fairness of the application of a zoning ordinance in specific cases and can contribute to the equal treatment of persons similarly situated. In zoning as in the administration of labor law what matters is whether like situations are treated alike, and whether a citizen can reasonably predict what the public response will be to his private acts. The comprehensive municipal plan is a useful technique to achieve these ends. To the citizen or landowner, the content of the plan is no more important than is the function of the plan to assure openness, predictability, and impartiality in the public decisions that implement the plan. The plan is good or bad as it permits the layman to check the consistency or irresponsibility of public decisions in specific cases. Equal protection is an essential principle of public administration whether the administrators are concerned with land development, public utilities, or liquor licenses.

These elementary prerequisites of acceptable public administration are not, however, the only principles which matter in land-use planning. The existence of a municipal plan is not enough. A limitation upon private decisions is justifiable only when the general welfare requires it, and "general welfare" is not a phrase first invoked by courts to measure the reasonableness of municipal zoning ordinances. Municipal boundaries probably are not coextensive with a welfare that is truly general. If this is so, then the invocation of a municipal plan as a basis for blocking a private decision may be illegitimate because it is beyond the scope of the "police power," that magic phrase invoked to justify government regulation over private decisions.

Other fundamental principles have their application in land-use planning. The current controversy between subdivision developers and municipalities over required dedication of open space for parks or schools as a precondition to approval of a subdivision plan does not pose a principle unique to land-use planning. What is placed on the table is the ancient dispute over where the police power (regulation without compensation) ends and eminent domain steps in. (If the public takes, the public pays.) We accept mandatory dedication of land for local streets necessary to serve the subdivision, but many courts regard compulsory dedication of land for public schools as overreaching by the municipality. In the former case it is plain that the requirement is a cost which should be borne only by the buyers of land in the subdivision. In the latter case we find it unacceptable to throw on these few taxpayers the cost of a public facility (schools) which benefits the entire municipality. The principle at issue is no more unique to zoning than it is to a score of other areas where the sovereign's right to regulate without compensation is challenged on the ground that the sovereign must invoke its right to condemn.

I mentioned procedural due process—a fair and expeditious hearing—as an example of valid and universal principle to be distinguished from a mere technique or goal of zoning. The indictment of zoning to which all critics subscribe is that its administration is arbitrary and capricious. Procedural due process is continually flaunted in our medieval hearings, our casual record keeping and our occult decision-making. I believe it is a greater social and political evil to have a "good" municipal plan from the viewpoint of design and physical content but to administer it unfairly than it is to have no plan but fair administration of a zoning ordinance. In my hierarchy of values procedural due process is a principle which in every case and to every man has substantially the same meaning. It is bunkum to maintain that there is a clear right and wrong in housing design or housing density, for example, and in the same breath to pontificate that "fairness" is an equivocal term which is useless as a principle for measuring municipal practices in regulating land use.

Fair procedure is a principle worth standing on. It has always escaped me why it should be applicable to the regulation of utilities and the administrative evaluation of commercial trade practices and not be equally valid in the arena of land-use policy. (Its relevance obviously has escaped many makers of local land-use policy.) Administrative fairness will serve as an acceptable and understandable principle in land-use policy as it does in utility regulation or the scrutiny of trade practices long after the exclusive single-family district, original cost versus fair value, and the quantity discount are displayed in the museums alongside the artifacts of Ur.

Zoning does itself a disservice when it goes beyond these catholic rules of conduct in its search for principles and tries to dignify its techniques, objectives, devices, and goals with more pretentious labels. This practice discourages necessary change in techniques to meet changes in demand. The voters as well as the courts have a considerable reluctance to repudiate a technique they have been taught to look upon as a principle.

As a matter of solace for the planners who demand a planning principle in the cloak of a non-principle, I can offer a couple of rules of thumb. First, there will be new demands for land use and new techniques for dealing with these demands; and, second, we cannot predict what form or scope either the demands or techniques will take. The herculean job of the planner, aware of the clouded condition of his crystal ball, is to accept these two rules and to try to figure out how the inevitable shifts in today's demands and the obsolescence of today's techniques can be absorbed at minimum social and economic cost.

The death of the street railway was relatively painless, if one puts out of mind the bondholders: four inches of macadam and the funeral was over. What remained to haunt the planners were the endless strips of commercial zones along the arteries that once carried the street car. The death struggle after World War II of the gabled twelve-room house in the 1910 subdivision has been ugly: the nursing home is not yet a wholly acceptable substitute even to the community that is wracked by tax delinquencies. In 1980 it will be more costly to eradicate the blighted tract subdivision built in 1950 than it will be to redevelop the land now occupied by everyone's pariah, the trailer park. Somebody should be "planning" in anticipation of this dreadful circumstance. Then there is the shopping center. Walter Blucher's suggestion that all shopping centers be designed for easy conversion to community recreation centers reflects a sensitivity to technological change. Electronics hold out the prospect to the housewife that she may once again do her shopping from her telephone, and the shopping center may be as obsolete as the strip commercial zone.

It will clear the air if we all concede that it does not denigrate land planning to acknowledge that while it has, from time to time, its own unique and useful techniques, its continuing validity in a democratic society is to be judged by the same general principles that are employed in other areas of the law. Then we can get on to the more difficult job of identifying the appropriate interests who are entitled to invoke these principles in land-use disputes.

IX

The Interested Parties

"Love your neighbor, but don't pull down the hedge."
Swiss Proverb

IT is one thing to suggest principles by which to measure the validity of land-use regulation. It is less clear who should be entitled to plead those principles and how they shall be applied in particular cases.

As I suggested in Chapter VII, one difficulty with the Planning Theory of zoning is that it assumes that the debate over land development is only between the landowner and the municipality. Both these parties do have a legitimate stake. The error in the present posture of the law is that many zoning disputes ignore other valid interests such as those of the region; or, as so frequently happens, the immediate neighbors are permitted to invoke the constitutional power of the municipality to achieve what are in fact only private ends. It is about time that the legitimate interests of all these parties—landowner, neighbor, municipality, and region—be redefined.

THE LANDOWNER

Few would dispute that the landowner is entitled to say to the municipality: if you prohibit all private use of my property, you must pay. The zoning ordinance must, for example, allow some reasonable use of the "undersized" but prerecorded and isolated lot, or the municipality must buy it. The landowner has a right to expect that the regulations will treat him the same as others similarly situated: he should not be subject to a thirty-five-foot setback when identical neighboring lots are built upon with fifteen-foot setbacks.

Equal treatment and some usability of the land are fair limitations on public regulation when the only valid interests at stake are those of landowner and municipality. It does not follow, however, that the landowner may insist on devoting his property to any use so long as it does not cause injury to the property of his neighbors. The law should consider the impact of the proposed land use not only on the neighbors but upon a broader spectrum of interests. The municipality must consider values beyond those of the neighbors' interests. So also the property owner is entitled to demand that the zoning restriction be validated by something more than the tastes of his neighbors or the social convictions of his community. Nor should the municipality be entitled to plead a burden on public services as a basis for rejecting a proposed development if the costs of those services are in fact spread beyond the boundaries of the municipality that regulates the use of the land. There are circumstances where the landowner's ambitions are in conflict with those of his neighbors but may be consistent with the interests of the metropolis. The one-acre minimum zoning of many fringe suburbs may not only frustrate the economic goals of the developer but may also impose additional costs upon the transportation system in the metropolitan area. The rejection of apartments by most suburbs can be viewed as a rejection of a promoter's desire for larger profits. It may also be a cause of higher cost of public services to the entire metropolis. As the London merchant and the Crown found common cause against the feudal nobles, so, in the next decade, the entrepreneur and the metropolis may find common purpose against the parochialism of the village. (This explains why the contemporary developer, like the draftsman of the Magna Charta, frequently talks like an unreconciled amalgamation of a fuzzy-minded liberal and a medieval land baron.)

THE NEIGHBOR

The boundaries of the neighbor's valid interests are blurred. (The "neighbor" is he who protests a proposed rezoning from, say, single-family to apartment or from single-family to commercial.) The neighbor's legal position as an objector to a rezoning proposal is tenuous. Generally he cannot invoke his position as a taxpayer to protest the grant of a development right (rezoning). He does not, for example, have the standing he enjoys as a taxpayer when he protests the expenditure of public funds. We have tended to invoke a rule of physical proximity that determines the right of a neighbor to protest a zoning change: if he lives in the same block he probably has standing to object; if he is five blocks away he cannot complain. This yardstick is evident in the customary statutory provision that requires more than a simple legislative majority to approve a rezoning petition if owners of adjacent land protest. In the judicial decisions this precept is cloaked with appropriate labels such as "special damages" that make it difficult for any but the closest neighbors to appeal to court development grants by municipalities. The judicial reluctance to extend the scope of private challenge to land-use decisions by municipalities reflects the customary judicial view that zoning changes affect only a very small geographical area. Undoubtedly this judicial resistance to third-party protest also prevents additional zoning cases on the dockets of the reviewing courts. The British administrative rule which denies to third parties the right to appeal to the Ministry from a grant of a development right has the same pragmatic root.

In spite of these rules that limit the right of the neighbor to protest zoning changes, the neighbor is often the real party in interest in land-use disputes that appear to be only between the petitioner and the municipality. The neighbor-objector who finds the door shut to him in the courts frequently takes the place of the community at the level of the local administrative hearing. The municipality speaks but the voice is that of the neighbor; he replaces the village as the adversary. In these cases—which represent a substantial percentage of zoning disputes—the role of the municipal agency ceases to be one of weighing the best interests of the entire community and becomes that of a referee between private parties, the petitioning landowner and his neighbors. This may be a reasonable consequence when the debate involves a request for a minor variance to a side yard, but it is hardly appropriate when the stake is a large-scale rezoning. These battles between landowner and neighbors are where we get the epithets of "government by screaming" and "trial by neighborism." It is a rare municipal legislature that will reject what it believes to be the wishes of the neighbors. The abdication to the neighbor of decision-making by the municipal legislature is particularly evident in the doctrine of "aldermanic courtesy" under a ward system. In such cases zoning decisions in theory are made by the municipal councils in the name of the city, but in fact are governed by the wishes of a single legislator speaking for his neighborhood constituents. This abdication of responsibility by the local government to neighborhood groups makes a sham of the presumption of validity that we grant to municipal legislation.

No doubt the neighbor does have some valid interests that are entitled to protection. Protection from the common law nuisance (whether in the form of a backyard hen house or a noisy window air conditioner) is the minimum he is entitled to expect. If the landowner proposes to erect dwelling units in a style other than single-family detached units, the neighbor should have the right to insist that there be provided the equivalents of the open space and light that would exist if the single-family, detached dwelling style had been maintained. The neighbor can insist on protection from the hazards of contagion and fire, and from the use of residential streets for four-axle trucks. Today the litany of zoning gives the neighbor a great deal more, including uniformity of housing design and housing type, simply for the sake of uniformity. I have never understood what the public welfare has to do with the style of housing my neighbor builds. I may not like it and if I sold him the land I can, at the time of sale, limit his perversity by private covenants. But, if he decides to go crazy modern or build a duplex but maintain the single-family density, it is beyond me why I should be able to call down constitutional imperatives to stop him.

Our attitudes toward the conflict between neighbor and neighbor over zoning can be tested by our feelings about the introduction of commercial uses into residential areas.

There has always been a small crack in the wall we have erected around the single-family district to insulate it against commercial intrusion: most communities have been willing to permit limited "self-help" occupations to be carried on in residential neighborhoods. These are commonly identified in zoning ordinances as "home occupations." A "home occupation" is a commercial use in a house that does not appear to change the primary residential character. A seamstress, a beauty shop, a real estate broker, a lawyer, a commercial artist, a widow selling antiques—any of these might be a home occupation. I have always wondered whether the choice of these commercial exceptions to the residential character have been based as much upon a careful analysis of the objectionable physical impact of particular non-residential uses upon residential neighborhoods as they have been on some unstated social attitudes toward particular non-residential uses. Neighborhood attitudes toward the accessory use of a residence for a beauty shop, a lawyer's office, a mom-and-dad food store or a casual dressmaker's operation depend not only upon preexisting conditions in the community but also upon the value judgments of the residents.

Generally, the scope of permitted "home occupations" in zoning ordinances reflects a social judgment that first says: it is not harmful to my status to have a professional office in my neighborhood and, at the other end of the scale, suggests that it is perfectly genteel for the widow Caruthers to make out with a little hemstitching in her parlor. But—and this is clear from the definitions in most ordinances—a beauty shop or a mom-and-dad gro-

cery store is unacceptable. Why this distinction? Our reaction seems
to depend on the particular test we use. Is the yardstick to be convenience, or traffic hazards, external appearance, or economic impact on the tax base of the already established commercial area?
Or is it none of these but a conviction that some non-residential
intrusions do not damage the "character" of the residential neighborhood irrespective of their impact on public services. If the test
were convenience to the neighbors, the beauty shop would be
more acceptable than the lawyer's or broker's office, and the
mom-and-dad grocery in the front of a house with its liberal
credit policy and its willingness to cater to special tastes and to
odd hours would justify first consideration. Not Jane Jacobs but
a planner said:

> Nothing is wrong with the old neighborhood grocery. And this
> troubles me because I can't find a decent way to put it in my zoning
> ordinance. And I want to save one. It's unique and provides the
> best cheese in the world. And you can buy beer on Saturday night
> when every supermarket is closed.

Nor can we explain our attitudes toward these small commercial intrusions into residential areas by reference to the hazards of
commercial traffic in a residential neighborhood. If our test was
based on traffic annoyance, the church would be the first to be
excluded from the residential district. Indeed, any "home occupation" which depended on and stimulated vehicular traffic would
not remain in the residential area, but would locate in areas
accessible to large scale traffic movement.

What I am saying is that we should stop the pretense that our
treatment of home "occupations" and other commercial intrusions
in residential areas is based on "planning" considerations. Our attitudes are grounded on very practical administrative, political, and
social considerations. It is easier to prohibit substantially all commercial activities in residential areas than it is to write and execute
provisions that would authorize that occasional special cheese
store or quaint antique shop. Absolute prohibition paradoxically
seems to involve less government control than does detailed regu-

lation that would permit, under a complex of considerations, some unique commercial uses. If this is so, then we should cut out the nonsense that our zoning practices in this area are based on "planning" factors, or upon some constitutional litany.

So let us admit that the neighbor has an interest that is entitled to be represented. My objection to his present dominant position in these disputes is that, as in the case of our attitude toward commercial intrusions, we have confused practical administrative considerations and social premises with constitutional imperatives and planning principles. This confusion has led, in turn, to an exaggerated attention to the neighborhood as the yardstick by which the validity or invalidity of a municipal regulation is measured.

(3) THE MUNICIPALITY

Traditionally the municipality has been the governmental unit which has represented the "public interest" in land-use decisions. The municipality today is predominant, and in many cases this is appropriate. The village has a direct interest in the weight of vehicles which use the residential streets that are paid for, maintained by, and primarily used by local residents. The village has a valid if not an exclusive interest in fire protection. If the village is responsible for the disposal within its boundaries of sanitary and industrial waste and garbage, its invocation of these considerations in any dispute over land use may also be valid. The village may be the logical and sole decision-maker when it comes to identifying those business uses whose presence in the central shopping area will destroy the vitality of that area. To the extent that property in the village pays the school costs, the impact of a proposed land development on school facilities may be a legitimate consideration.

I would be willing to let the municipalities represent the general welfare in those cases where either the grant of development, the particular conditions under which it occurs, or the denial of it, does not place a significant burden upon other public interests.

In land-use disputes that have little if any impact outside municipal boundaries, it may be sufficient that the local residents desire a particular physical character. All that matters is that if A and B share like circumstance, A and B be treated alike. If Golden Bough Center opts to omit curbs and gutters in its subdivisions but insists that all plats make maximum use of the cul-de-sac, what cares East Golden Bough? If Glenfield, with a penchant for quaintness, believes it makes civic sense to require all business properties to sport facades that will give shoppers the feeling that they are in Stratford-on-Avon, and to insist that no two houses in a residential block be of the same design, this quixotic municipal pastime will probably have no overwhelming impact on metropolitan policy. The silliness represented by the "look-alike" ordinance and the "non-look-alike" ordinance, resting side by side in the same municipal code, may be cause for amusement but not for concern within the metropolitan area; unless, that is, the current call for a national aesthetic renaissance results in beauty-by-committee. Then one is entitled to wonder what hope there is for the Frank Lloyd Wright of the next generation. The intermixing of business uses in residential neighborhoods, the design features of subdivisions and the treatment of neighborhood open space are other examples of local decisions that may have a *de minimis* impact upon other ants in the metropolitan hill. The exclusion of drive-in uses from prime retail districts, the limitation on variety in dwelling type (with no increase in density), and the standards for industrial uses may or may not have more than local significance.

THE METROPOLIS

"The last word," Alfred Bettman observed in 1927, "has not as yet been uttered on this question of the relationship of the metropolitan factor to the validity of specific zone plans."[1] Noting Justice Sutherland's passing distinction in the *Euclid* decision between the "general public interest" and "the interest of the municipality," Bettman continued:

This passage in the opinion is noteworthy in that it presents the conflict not as one between the individual and the community, but rather as between different communities, different social groups, or social interests, which is, when profoundly comprehended, true of all police power constitutional issues.

In many functions of urban life the responsibility of the village has been passed to the larger community of which the municipality is a part. Common to all those instances where local control has been abdicated are their asocial nature and their demonstrable impact upon private convenience or safety. The establishment of metropolitan sanitary systems is generally unchallenged not only because of the urgency to health but also because the social implications are too subtle or indirect to be readily grasped.

By contrast, the malevolent but delayed consequence of private septic systems to public health and the public budget is not as apparent to the resident in a minimum one-acre zone as are the immediate social implications of a small lot, tract subdivision with public sewer and water. Our attitudes toward metropolitan or state planning of highways reflect these same considerations although historical influences play a more dominant part here. We appear willing if not eager to vest responsibility for road building in political entities larger than the municipality. In the case of conflict between metropolitan or state interests in a highway location and a municipal plan, the odds are heavy against the survival of the local plan.

When it comes to the use of private land, however, there has been little room for metropolitan considerations in the pattern of our zoning and planning law. The common municipal attitude is expressed by these words of a plan commission chairman in a midwestern suburb: "We zoned industry right up to this Nickel Plate Railroad. With no consideration of the village of———at all. And on the other side of this railroad are some very high class residential developments. We never even talked to them. We just bang and did it. They don't like it but. . . ." Hugh Pomeroy put the standard this way: "If a community desires to maintain a secluded low density residential environment represented by detached houses on large parcels of land that reason alone is sufficient to sustain the determination to do so." On this premise there is no place in current debate over private land use for considerations beyond the boundaries of the municipality.

The observation of perceptive California builder Ed Eichler sums it up:

> At least if Palo Alto had said okay we're going to be a rural community and the hell with anything to do with the modernization of man, they would have been consistent. They didn't do that. They grabbed off all the good part and they hurt all of the other communities, as well as a lot of people, by their exclusionary practices.
>
> BABCOCK: Why couldn't the other communities have followed the same practice? How did Palo Alto hurt them?
>
> EICHLER: Palo Alto started it first.

In many instances the preeminence of the municipality is appropriate and is not inconsistent with the interests of the larger community. The scope of the general welfare invoked to enforce policy on the use of private land should be coextensive with the responsibility for providing the public services which benefit private land and whose efficiency is affected by the use of private land. If municipalities are going to look to the highways of the state to provide them convenience, to the sanitary systems of the metropolis to protect their residents' health, to the regional water resources to provide recreation, and to the federal government to help finance their open space acquisitions, the municipalities must also be prepared to have disputes over private land uses which may impinge upon the efficiency of those regional resources determined by something more than local criteria. If the communities are going to turn increasingly to the state, if not the nation, for aid to schools, then they should not be taken aback if the plea of the overburdened school against increased residential densities loses some of its appeal. If the local communities are willing to pass on to larger units the responsibility for policy-making in matters such as transportation, open space, sanitation, clean air, and water resources, that not only directly affect the value of private land but are themselves directly harmed or benefited by the use of private land, the municipalities should not be surprised if decision-making gravitates also to the larger community or, at the least, that the validity of their local decisions is measured by something other than the municipality's parochial goals. (It is inconceivable, for example, that the mounting political interest in air pollution will stop short of regional, if not national, regulation of the causes. This consequence will inevitably result in some transfer of control over industrial uses from municipal to more comprehensive governmental units.)

This abdication of fiscal responsibility by the municipality is why I have trouble with the homage paid the municipal plan by so many planners. In our society, where pluralistic, segmented, and fractured local political systems stand squared off against forces compelling the most intimate overall social and economic relationships, a municipal plan for a single political entity is not the ultimate test of legitimacy of local regulation. The hopes and fears of one municipality may be beside the point or they may be relevant when measured by some more broadly based purpose. Indeed, in a metropolitan area the words "comprehensive plan" are meaningless if not self-contradictory when applied to each of one hundred suburbs. Those courts that have been called upon to construe that seductive slogan, "comprehensive plan," in the standard state zoning enabling acts have been remarkably if unconsciously perceptive when they concluded that the phrase "in accordance with a comprehensive plan" meant no more than that the zoning ordinance embraced all the land in the municipality. "In accordance with a comprehensive plan" is far from being an infallible guide to legitimate municipal decision-making, and in each passing decade as we become cosmopolites in everything but our local political districts the "principle" becomes more fallible.

Examples of the stultification caused by a municipal land-use policy can be seen in the suburban attempt to prevent the construction of apartments through the use of exclusive single-family zoning, and the use of large-acreage zoning to discourage or avoid entirely more intense residential development. Nor am I persuaded by the customary cost-revenue arguments advanced by municipalities to justify their resistance to development.

One of the most troublesome aspects of the cost-revenue argument used to justify both large-lot and anti-apartment suburban zoning is that it begs the question.[2] It implies that each municipality has the right to reject increased density simply because development will require additional public services. Yet such a restrictive home-rule philosophy is now quite common. The economic and social mobility and the growth of American society is attributable in large part to the frontier psychology which insisted that the availability of public services follows the demand rather than controls it. Without this premise, we would never have crossed the Alleghenies. The early history of the United States shows a continuous, deeply-rooted policy of encouraging growth and expansion. If the Homestead Act had permitted settlement of the West only upon the consent of the existing residents, the Indians might have been happier, but this would be a much different country today.

This does not mean that unrestricted growth and expansion can be our only policy. Even in the century of manifest destiny, the national parks and forests were restricted to low-density development. But growth and expansion should be the rule, the restriction and exclusion the exception. Any community which wishes to retain low-density development should be required to show why, among all the towns in the region, it deserves to be set aside as a low-density reservation. Perhaps it can point to drainage or transportation problems which would justify restrictive policies as a matter of sound regional planning; perhaps it cannot. But the fact is that in most states today a community does not need to cite regional considerations to justify its restrictive policies on density because neither the legislatures nor the courts have required it.

If each separate community may plead an alleged strain on public services as a basis for rejection of greater density, then we have, indeed, repudiated those theses on which this continent was developed, and have returned full circle to a medieval society, granting exclusive corporate franchises based upon a municipal primogeniture. If each town's crowded schools, overtaxed sewers, or inadequate streets are sufficient bases for excluding a use of land which will increase the municipal burden, then we have subscribed to the principle that what has been done is the legal justification for what shall be done. On this reasoning, the prudent school district must accept the pressure of heavier density, while the spendthrift district can plead inability to meet the added cost. The community which has enshrined its xenophobia in a "master plan" has demonstrated a skill in "one-upmanship" that will be the envy of its more lethargic municipal neighbors. The rural community can validly refuse to accept a share of the centrifugal explosion, but the municipality closer to the urban core which has come too late to the planning banquet may have no legal basis for refusal. In short, if the inadequacy of local public services, without any consideration of the broader regional problems, is a defense to a petition for greater density, we will have contributed to the already distorted pattern of metropolitan growth.

If the legitimate interests of the metropolis or state are relevant in many land use disputes, there will remain scores of contests where the only appropriate issues are between owner and neighbor or owner and municipality. Admittedly, it will not be an easy task to distinguish the case with only a local significance from that which has wider consequences.

The fact that the non-local consequences may be difficult to predict or establish in these gray areas does not mean that their relevance should not be permitted to be demonstrated and evaluated: does the county or region have an interest that merits consideration by the court or the state legislature in a dispute between a promoter who wants to build five thousand homes on quarter-acre lots and a municipality which wants to maintain its one-acre minimum bucolic character? Or, to put it another way, should the county or region have a right to be heard if the promoter and the municipality agree that five thousand homes should be constructed where formerly only one thousand would have been permitted? It is hard to conceive how such convulsive change will not have repercussions outside the municipality upon public facilities and resources that are supported by greater numbers than will participate in the local decision. The emasculation of regional transportation, water resources, recreational or sanitary systems may be the consequence of the particular development. If the community persists in its goals, the population explosion from the metropolitan core will leapfrog at far greater cost to the highway system. As William Whyte says "the community does not get penetrated; it gets enveloped." Perhaps none of these potentials will turn out to apply to this dispute. Today in our approach to land-use debates, there is not even an opportunity to consider whether such non-municipal interests are material or not.

One practical difficulty blocking such an outlook is that of mechanics. In zoning litigation how and by whom is the regional interest to be presented? I see no great hazard to allowing either of the traditional parties to invoke this broader concept of public welfare. If it is self-serving for the developer to wrap his proposal in the cloth of regional considerations it will not be the first time public goals have been used to shore up individual ambitions. If the municipality appears a bit hypocritical in its invocation of regional interests, such an attempt to dignify parochial objectives does not invalidate the regional considerations which support the municipal interests. Nor should there be any reason why direct intervention by other municipalities or by private or public associations concerned with metropolitan land use should not be permitted. If, as I suggest in Chapter X, a state planning agency or board should have review powers over zoning disputes, there is no reason why the staff of that agency could not raise metropolitan issues.

The sole test of the materiality of evidence in zoning disputes should not be whether the offered proof is related only to municipal rights and interests. The issue may not, as it turns out, raise a question that requires the arbiter to harken to a voice outside the municipality. In such a case, the inappropriateness of the intervention or offer of proof is for the arbiter to determine. This is a burden greater only in degree than that put upon judges in current zoning disputes when they are called upon to determine the relevance of existing uses within the neighborhood.

It seems clear, however, that the legitimate interests of those outside the municipality are not going to be heard until we have a major revision of state legislation in the field of land-use regulation.

X

The Bases for Decision-Making

"It is obvious that Valley View, Ohio, is . . . only an adventitious fragment of the economic and social whole."
Valley View Village v. Proffett,
221 F.2d 412

UNDER any politically acceptable system for resolving disputes over the use of privately owned land, the municipality
will probably retain its role as initial decision-maker. The state will
increasingly influence decisions on private land use where major
public services are affected, and the federal government will insin-
uate itself into this arena by use of its traditional cash carrot.
Nevertheless, there will remain thousands of disputes over the use
of private land in which the exercise of judgment will be vested
exclusively in municipal bodies.

This is as it should be. Yet even if the decision-making remains
local it is appropriate, in those cases where the dispute may raise
issues beyond that of neighbor versus neighbor or may impose
costs beyond the municipal boundaries, that the criteria for the
decision should be consistent with the interests of the region. The
error in zoning today is not that the decision-making is exclusively
municipal; the flaw is that the *criteria* for decision-making are
exclusively local, even when the interests affected are far more
comprehensive.

Reform in current land-use policy will require a substantial
change in our state enabling acts along three lines: (1) more
detailed statutory prescription of the required administrative pro-

153

cedures at the local level; (2) a statutory restatement of the major substantive criteria by which the reasonableness of local decision-making is measured; (3) the creation of a state-wide administrative agency to review the decisions of local authorities in land-use matters, with final appeal to an appellate court. These reforms require that a distinction be made between procedural matters and those of substance; between control over the manner in which decisions on land use are made and the basis of the decisions themselves.

STATUTORY CONTROL OVER MUNICIPAL PROCEDURES

On procedure in land-use decision-making, I speak of matters dear to the lawyer and of infinite boredom to the planner: local record keeping, the conduct of the local hearing, and the adequacy of the findings of the local administrative agency. This is the Sargasso Sea of zoning. It is pretense to invite the architects and planners to argue the respective flaws and benefits of two competing development proposals before we have made clear to each applicant that the same rules will apply to each. Before we can indulge in the luxury of debate on design in our cities, we have to face up to the issue of fair play in municipal administration. An earlier observation of mine is still valid:

> The running, ugly sore of zoning is the total failure of this system of law to develop a code of administrative ethics. Stripped of all planning jargon, zoning administration is exposed as a process under which multitudes of isolated social and political units engage in highly emotional altercations over the use of land, most of which are settled by crude tribal adaptations of medieval trial by fire, and a few of which are concluded by confused *ad hoc* injunctions of bewildered courts.[1]

The local administrative practices vary from some resemblance to rules for judicial hearings to the most colloquial proceedings. In too many municipalities the local tribunal looks upon itself as an advocate for a point of view. The petition of one aggrieved property owner to court (where the local decision was reversed) alleged that at the opening of the local hearing on his request for a rezoning:

> The Chairman of said Macon County Zoning Board of Appeals thereupon made a speech for the gathering, stating that if this rezoning was permitted that it would open the door for garages, taverns and all sorts of undesirable businesses to be located upon said property; that when certain of the property owners reminded the speaker that the township was dry, he corrected himself.[2]

One zoning board may insist upon a transcribed verbatim record of the proceedings, another board may be content with a pro forma record. Some administer oaths, others do not. In some instances it is hard to distinguish the attorney from the witnesses. Counsel "testifies" as much as his clients. In one town the unverified petition of neighbors is the principal basis for decision-making; down the pike no value is attached to the petition. In one community the applicant has a chance to cross-examine the planner who has commented to the local body on the merits of the application, in another the planner's opinions are not available to the applicant. In some instances a board will refer to "evidence" not put in the formal record, hence denying the parties a chance to challenge the relevance of that part of the "record." Some places follow a code strict enough to satisfy the most sensitive conscience in disqualifying a board member because of conflict; in more relaxed jurisdictions, personal involvement by a hearing official is a matter of indifference. The casual attitude among local boards toward the content of the required "findings of fact" is notorious. Most of them simply regurgitate the vague guidelines set out in the state enabling act.

The record-keeping is frequently just as execrable. In too many instances, it is difficult, if not impossible, to dig out the existing local regulations. There may be a published ordinance but it may have been modified by a disorganized pile of amendments found only in the third drawer of the village clerk's desk.

It is inconceivable to me that the bench can clear up this mishmash of municipal zoning administration. Judicial surveillance of local procedure under our present enabling legislation is ineffectual. A reversal or remand by the courts because of sloppy procedure before the board of appeals of Broadview has not, in my experience, the slightest impact on the practices of neighboring Westchester. Furthermore, the costs of procedural rule-making by the bench are intolerable. Attorney Frederick Stickel's description of the way things work in New Jersey is applicable in other jurisdictions:

> We've had several of our most important decisions of our Supreme Court where property owners have been put to the expense of a proceeding before the Board of Adjustment, proceeding before the governing body, then a review of both actions by the superior court, an appeal to the appellate division, a split-decision in the appellate division and an appeal to the Supreme Court and then a decision by the Supreme Court that the findings were inadequate and a remand and start all over again. To my way of thinking this is not only an imposition upon the taxpayers who have to foot the expense of all these appeals and proceedings but as a lawyer I think it is an imposition to the average property-owner. I don't think the average property-owner can afford anything of that nature. And when he's faced with something like this he just gives up at the local level because he can't afford to go through, either from a point of time or expense, anything like this. And to have these cases get all the way up to the Supreme Court and then have them find an inadequate record and a remand to my way of thinking is just a terrific imposition on everybody. As much as the courts have, in their opinions, tried to educate Board of Adjustment and governing bodies and even municipal attorneys, they haven't broken through.

The attempts of the Illinois Supreme Court to bring some sense of procedural responsibility to local practices in that state have been just as fruitless. In 1956 the court said it was not sufficient for a local board to "parrot" the statutory standards when passing upon a request for a variance.[3] There is little evidence that this injunction has been taken seriously by Illinois municipalities.

Only the legislature can prescribe adequate rules for local administrative procedure and record-keeping, by more detailed statutory directives and, as suggested below, by the creation of a statewide administrative agency with the power to review local procedures. It is reasonable to expect, from municipality to municipality, differences in substantive goals and objectives, and it is not essential to procedural due process that there be uniformity in procedure among the hundreds of municipalities in each state. But substantial uniformity of local procedure will be an inevitable consequence of an insistence by the state that each community that elects to regulate land use maintain a procedural system that contributes to fairness and openness in local administration. I had occasion recently to work on a model section of an enabling act on procedure at the local public hearing. The language treated in part at least of some of these matters:

1. The local agency shall publish the rules to govern the hearing so that every interested party shall know in advance the procedures under which a hearing shall be conducted.

2. Technical rules of evidence are not applicable to the hearing but the local agency shall exclude irrelevant, immaterial, or unduly repetitious evidence and such evidence as is not of the kind which would affect reasonable men in the conduct of their daily affairs.

3. All witnesses intending to speak in favor of or opposed to a proposed amendment, variance, or exception shall be sworn under oath by the chairman and the right of cross-examination shall be available to every party. No petitions signed by persons not present at the hearing shall be admitted into evidence except by stipulation of all parties to the hearing.

4. No finding by the local agency shall be made except as it is based upon evidence introduced at said hearing or upon official records of the municipality or other public agency that are available to the public.

5. A transcript of the testimony at the hearing shall be made, copies of which shall be available at cost to any party who requests the same. All exhibits accepted in evidence shall be identified and duly preserved, or, if not accepted in evidence shall

be properly identified and the reason for the exclusion clearly noted in the record.

6. When there is a municipal planning staff the municipal authority shall require that any report by the staff on the application be placed on public record prior to the hearing.

7. The local agency shall support its conclusions by findings of fact and shall recite with particularity the reasons for its conclusions in the specific case before it.

These rules do not distinguish between the case where the local hearing is conducted by an appointed "administrative" agency and that where the local legislature itself conducts the hearing. The lawyer may find this disturbing, accustomed as he is to believe that the legislature, unlike an "administrative" agency, is not required to explain its actions or to follow quasi-judicial procedures. (I question whether the traditional "separation of powers" doctrine has any validity, historically or legally, at the level of municipal government.) The freedom from accountability of the municipal governing body may be tolerable in those cases where the legislature is engaged in legislating but it makes no sense where the legislature is dispensing or refusing to dispense special grants. When the local legislature acts to pass general laws applicable generally it is performing its traditional role and it is entitled to be free from those strictures we place upon an agency that is charged with granting or denying special privileges to particular persons. When the municipal legislature crosses over into the role of hearing and passing on individual petitions in adversary proceedings it should be required to meet the same procedural standards we expect from a traditional administrative agency.

The irony of our failure to effect a statutory cure for the administrative chaos in zoning is that it is politically feasible. Few would protest a statutory command to give a fair hearing provided the statute does not prescribe the outcome of the hearing. Neither would it appear unreasonable for the state to provide that no zoning ordinance, nor any amendment thereto, shall be effective until it is filed of record in the office of the county clerk, thereby making it possible to determine just what the zoning is at any given time.

Among the indirect rewards of such procedural directives would be a significant improvement in substantive policy that may be, as a political matter, less susceptible of direct cure. If the state legislature insists that, whatever municipalities decide to do as a substantive matter, they shall follow a carefully prescribed procedure, the consequence will be that capricious action will be more readily exposed to the agency charged with the duty to review. The cloak for arbitrary decision-making is the absence of any command to follow uniform practice, to explain, and to make a record. If little or nothing is put on the record by the municipal agency, the less the chance of reversal. The courts continually fume over this endemic condition in zoning practice but, absent any statutory imperatives, the bench generally either has felt no obligation or has found no method to cure the condition. The planning profession has no apparent interest in administration and, in any event, is not qualified to act. The unhappy state of zoning administration is clearly the responsibility of the bar and of the state legislatures.

(2) THE SUBSTANTIVE REFORM

The tough nut is to articulate substantive standards to evaluate all the legitimate interests concerned with land-use policy. There are more powerful oxen that would be gored by changes in the substantive criteria by which local zoning policy is validated than would be affected by administrative reform.

What is called for, after more than forty years under the 1925 Department of Commerce model act and its progeny, is to recast state enabling legislation to introduce new criteria for municipal planning policy, and to command local bodies to measure their decisions by those criteria. This does not remove from municipalities the initial responsibility to regulate; neither does it insist that a "plan" is a prerequisite to local regulation. The state legislature should, however, speak on those matters where the local body must consider the interests of the region or of the state. If the municipality does not, the reviewing body will. The state should, for example, set forth in the statute whether the reasonableness (validity) of local decisions affecting land adjacent to state highways and navigable waters will be determined in part by the impact of the proposed use on those regional resources. The state should articulate whether the reasonableness of local decisions over density of development will be determined, in part at least, by the impact of a chosen density (whether high-rise apartments or minimum three-acre) upon metropolitan transportation. The state should articulate in the enabling act what significance, if any, the impact of development on public schools shall have in a land-use dispute. The state should express policy on the appropriateness of public control over architectural design: for example, that it is not a subject of either municipal or regional concern except in areas the legislature declares to be of historic significance. The state should indicate whether a decision to mix or not mix commercial and residential uses is solely a matter of policy for the local community: are metropolitan considerations relevant to a determination of the validity of municipal regulation in such cases? The state should say whether a particular subject of land-use development is or is not of more than municipal concern. Is the dispute solely one of concern to landowner and municipality or does the state or region also have an interest at stake?

Each municipality would be directed to set forth the manner in which its ordinance complied with those legislative criteria. In cases where requests are made for changes in land-use regulations, the local body would have to weigh not only the traditional "neighborhood" considerations but also these new and more comprehensive statutory considerations in making its decision. The reviewing body would pass judgment not only in the light of the old parochial values but also with these new statutory guidelines in mind.

The dialogue between a new zoning enabling act and a local zoning ordinance might go somewhat as follows in various areas of land-use policy. These examples are not intended to cover the full range of land-use issues on which the state should speak. (The statute is speaking to those matters of policy that the local ordinance must consider):

PROPOSED

On Transportation

> *Enabling Act.* The municipal ordinance shall: . . . Encourage that use of land adjacent to major transportation arteries, financed in whole or substantial part by non-municipal funds, that shall contribute to the efficient and economical use of these facilities throughout the entire area they are designed to serve.

This statement advises municipalities they must consider something more than their own local interests, and it permits courts or administrative agencies to admit metropolitan considerations in their evaluation of disputes involving the use of land adjacent to major vehicular arteries. Whether those responsible for building the highways must, in turn, recognize the interests of the localities should also be considered by the state.

Ordinance in Community A. Community A has a limited-access highway and a major four-lane, non-limited-access highway passing through its territory. It must state in its plan or ordinance what its objectives are with respect to the use of land along these arteries. It must further state in what way its regulation of the use of land adjacent to these arteries does contribute to a more efficient and economical use of these facilities. If a decision to rezone for an industry or a shopping center at an interchange impedes these facilities, the municipality must state what other considerations warranted such an impediment. The reviewing body, administrative or judicial, has a statutory basis for evaluating the reasonableness of the municipal action, not solely in terms of the loss to the landowner versus gain to the municipality but in terms of the impact upon a non-municipal asset.

Ordinance in Community B. This community has no such major traffic arteries. It is a leafy, lakeside residential community. Arterial traffic passes around it. This particular objective in the enabling act has no present application to the community, and it says so in its plan or ordinance.

On Water

> *Enabling Act.* The municipal ordinance shall: . . . Recognize the interest of all the citizens of the state in the conservation and efficient use of the public lakes and rivers for recreation, a clean water supply and other public needs, and the regulation of the use of land adjacent to said lakes and rivers shall not only consider the existing use of land adjacent to such resources but shall take into consideration the impact of the expansion of such existing use and of any new or different use upon the needs of the entire region served by those resources.

Ordinance of Community A. It has no public lakes or rivers within its boundaries. It passes.

Ordinance of Community B. A major river bisects Community B and half the border of a large lake is within the municipality. The town has some small industry, an obsolescent power generating plant, and the beginnings of a recreation boom. This town has problems. Fortunately the enabling act requires that it take a hard look at itself, decide what it wants to be, and how that decision will affect the other communities who depend on the resources represented by the lake and the river. Will a rezoning to permit relocation of the power plant on the river or the expansion of the industrial zone without adequate controls over effluent into the river spoil downstream recreation in another community? Can municipal resistance to an increase in the density of riparian summer cottages be sustained, against protest of developers, on the ground that the municipality recognizes its obligation to the entire river basin and additional densities will jeopardize the downstream use of the river? Or, if the developer proposes an efficient sewerage disposal system, could he then point to the interest of the region in providing additional recreation facilities?

Patently the articulation of criteria in the statute would not provide rote answers to any land-use dispute involving riparian land. But it would offer a less parochial basis by which the reasonableness of local decisions can be measured. The debate would have more meaning in the last half of the twentieth century.

On Architectural Design

Enabling Act. The municipal ordinance shall: . . . Permit that variety and scope of architectural design which will encourage the development of individual taste and imagination, provided, however, limitation upon design shall be permitted where it can be shown that (a) the regulation has a direct relation to the efficiency of public services, or (b) the regulation is intended to protect and encourage an established architectural character that has an historical significance and an economic benefit to the municipality or to the metropolitan area of which it is a part.

In this case the legislature has determined that architectural control is no business of the public except in rare instances where, for example, fire safety is related to design or where, as in the case of the Vieux Carré or Beacon Hill, there is a demonstrable nexus between style and historical preservation. Under this type of statute, the "look-alike" ordinance as well as the "non-look-alike" ordinance of the postwar suburb is out. Here the legislature has opted for the property owner, no matter how eccentric he may be.

The legislature might, on the other hand, under the pervasive influence of suburbia, decide that architectural design, having no significant impact on regional resources or regional costs, may be left to the whim of each municipality. In such case the statute might read as follows:

Enabling Act. The municipal ordinance *may:* . . . Make such provision for the regulation of architectural style or design, based upon historical development or the prevailing architectural style in the municipality as shall be deemed by the municipality to assure the preservation of the character of the municipality, provided, however, that no local regulation over architectural design shall constitute an undue interference with those services or facilities which are a responsibility of and benefit to the region of which the municipality is a part.

In this case each municipality is free to do as it pleases and the odd-ball builder has no complaint except in the unlikely event that rigid architectural specifications have an adverse impact on regional interests. This means that taste is left to a committee, a rather dismal prospect, but here the individualist can no longer invoke the interests of the region to support his demand for greater freedom.

On Dwelling Type

> *Enabling Act.* The municipal ordinance shall: . . . Encourage variation and intermixing of dwelling types in substantially undeveloped areas in order to meet the demand for a variety in housing present in a metropolitan area without sacrifice to those reasonable amenities of open space and other neighborhood amenities, the protection of which are consistent with the mobility of persons in the metropolitan community.

This statement suggests a factor not present in current legislation and at the heart of the debate over cluster subdivisions. On the other hand, the statute could have made clear that segregation of dwelling type is a proper municipal function in which the region and state have no interest. At the least, the selection of the appropriate policy in this instance should be made by a broader constituency than is represented by each municipal government.

Ordinance in Community A. Community A insists upon maintaining its character as an area of detached, single-family houses. It states this as an objective and then states why it does not wish to encourage variety of dwelling types and why it believes this is not contrary to the general welfare of the metropolitan area. Whether this is a "legitimate" answer to the developer who wants to build row houses or apartments is for the referee (court or agency) to decide. At least the enabling act has spoken to the problem. It permits the issue of variety in dwelling type to be introduced. Today uniformity is regarded almost as a constitutional imperative.

Ordinance in Community B. Community B prefers to go to a "general" residential classification in large undeveloped areas where density per acre and not dwelling type is the basis for classification of the residential districts. It also elects to permit cluster subdivisions under specific conditions. It so states its policy, explains why some limitations are necessary, and sets out the objectives or goals that it expects to accomplish by this novel practice. Against attack by residents of detached dwellings it can point to the policy of the statute.

On Density

Enabling Act. The municipal ordinance shall: . . . Recognize the direct interest of the region of which the municipality is a part in the direction and intensity of the use of land for residential development and the impact, both adverse and beneficial, of particular densities of population upon regional transportation, recreation, and other public facilities; and, in the classification by intensity of use of land for residential development, take into consideration not only the particular topography and condition of the land, the use of neighboring property, and the impact upon local services, but also the impact, if any, upon the efficient allocation of the resources and public facilities of the entire region of which the municipality is a part; and in the regulation of densities base its decisions on other than a purpose to limit development to one economic or social class.

Ordinance in Community A. Community A desires to maintain three-acre zoning. Soil tests show this is not necessary to prevent pestilence. It must explain in its plan or ordinance why unusual topography may justify limiting development, or it may set forth that in fact it does have a specific program for more intense development in its prairie areas consistent with a specific program of public improvements. Or, it may allege that the decision to have exclusive three-acre zoning was reached after county-wide intergovernmental planning in which there had been a consensus among numerous municipalities that three-acre zoning was appropriate for Community A.

Ordinance in Community B. This is a community built up during the 1920's with many twenty-five foot wide lots. It now wishes to limit additional development—particularly in peripheral areas to be annexed—to larger lots. It describes its history, sets forth the problems relating to small lots, notes the change to ranch style houses, recognizes that it can do nothing with those ancient subdivisions, but develops a thesis in support of its objective to require larger lots for additional subdivision.

Neither these examples nor similar criteria hold out a precise yardstick for determining the reasonableness or unreasonableness of municipal action in a particular phase of land-use regulation. Exactitude is not only unrealistic but undesirable. These standards do represent an expression of state policy (or a decision to have no state policy) in particular categories of land use and this would be a major step toward a more rational resolution of the disputes between landowner, municipality- and region.

I have cast the voice of the state in the enabling statute itself. There certainly is room for debate whether these policy statements should be left to a state administrative agency of the sort I propose, rather than to appear in the statute itself. My own preference for statutory expression is based on a conviction that the legislature should not abdicate its political responsibility to articulate policy. In any event, in my scheme there still remains a wide area for implementation of policy by the state administrative agency.

THE STATE ADMINISTRATIVE AGENCY

Someone, either the courts or a state administrative agency, will have to determine the applicability of the statutory criteria in particular cases and will have to decide whether the local procedure is consistent with the statutory mandate. I doubt that the trial courts are equipped either to resolve the distressing condition of local zoning administration or to formulate state or regional policy in substantive matters. In forty years the judiciary has not done so because it cannot and, besides, does not want to. If municipal zoning administration were subject to a centralized administrative review, the appellate courts could in turn provide more certain control over administrative practices.

Justice Oliver Wendell Holmes observed that one of the most significant contributions of the federal system to the art of self-government was the opportunity for a state to serve as a laboratory in which new ideas in government could be tested. It is time some state, operating on such a premise, established a state-wide agency among whose duties would be the authority (1) to enforce a statutory mandate for uniform rules of procedure and standards of evidence for hearings before local zoning boards, commissions, and legislative committees; (2) to hear, under the policy criteria set out in the statute, all appeals from rulings of those local bodies that are vested with power to grant or deny variances, amendments, and special uses; and (3) in some instances to grant cash awards as a condition of sustaining local zoning policy. Such a system may be the only feasible solution to the chaos that characterizes this field of law.

The first of these powers would insure that every owner of real estate, wherever it was located, would be judged by similar standards and heard under identical procedures. Not the least of the merits of such a state-wide authority would be a wider dissemination of information among local administrative bodies. Such an agency could provide that glue of participation in a common administrative effort that is totally absent from zoning administration today despite the good intentions of various lay and professional organizations.

The legislature also directs the statewide commission to review local decision-making in terms of the broad criteria set out in the statute, as the state utilities commission is commanded to resolve disputes over utility rates in terms of a reasonable rate of return, either on the basis of current fair value or on original cost of the utility plant. Under such a system, the job of building a body of substantive law around the statutory skeleton is the duty of the agency. The legislature does no more than indicate those areas where "general welfare" is or is not coextensive with municipal boundaries.

There is one other function such an agency could perform: the awarding of damages in those tough cases where the fairest solution is to sustain the regulation but to compensate the landowner for the loss. One reason for the negative reaction of the bench toward zoning is that most judges realize many zoning cases are not black or white, that reason is not all on one side, but there is no machinery by which he can declare the zoning a "little bit invalid."

Because zoning litigation is an all-or-nothing proposition, the judge is constantly forced to make decisions in which he does not wholeheartedly believe. Either the city wins and the property owner is absolutely prevented from pursuing his development, or the city loses and the plaintiff achieves his objective regardless of the impact on the neighborhood or the community. This consequence is assumed to be inherent in a regulatory technique based on the police power. There has been no method developed by which in an adversary process the municipality's desire, for example, to limit development to residential use is sustained, but the landowner can get damages for the refusal of the municipality to allow him to use his property for commercial purposes. There has not been a place in American zoning law for an equivalent to the British concept of compensation (in theory full, in practice partial). In this country there is to be no area of compromise where the greater interests of the community are acknowledged but the consequence to the landowner is such that he receives a monetary compensation for what amounts to a partial taking of his property. Undoubtedly there are many cases where the all-or-nothing approach is appropriate. If a developer seeks to construct an industrial plant in a residential area accessible only by streets designed for non-industrial traffic, the denial of this ambition carries with it no concern that residential development will be unlikely. The petitioner's request is clearly unreasonable. At the other end of the scale, an attempt by the municipality to impose a single-family residential classification on a small enclave within a commercial area may appear so outrageous to any man (who is not a local resident) that the developer should be granted his petition irrespective of local desires. In such a case damages are not enough. Let him proceed.

In my experience, many zoning cases are not so obvious. As attorney for community or developer in a lawsuit, I have often wished for some judicial technique to impose an easement on the property which would limit the use to that intended by the municipality and for which limitation the village would pay. Two instances come to mind where the issue was treated as black or white and yet it was apparent that it was neither.

Thirty-five miles from Chicago two heavily traveled two-lane state highways intersect at a grade two miles from a suburban community. Back from the corners of the intersection in all directions there has been, during the past decade, substantial and expensive single-family development at very low densities. The acreage at three corners of the intersection has remained vacant under its minimum one-acre single-family classification despite the abutting residential growth in all directions. On one corner there is a commercial horse stable. The local government takes the position that it would be intolerable to permit commercial development at each of the vacant corners, and to sanction commercial development at one corner would inexorably lead to demands for similar uses at the other corners. The predominant residential area would be eroded. There appear to be valid considerations of traffic safety and existing residential values to back up this position. In view of substantial commercial centers within two miles, there seems to be little "need" for a small commercial complex.

The owner of the corner lot, on the other hand, can make a persuasive case that his property faces an impediment to residential development not imposed on his adjoining residential neighbors: traffic lights have not as yet gained acceptance as front yard ornaments. The single-family classification of the corner results, he insists, in a permanent dedication of his property as open space without compensation. Were I the judge in such a case, I would wish for some mechanism which would make available a middle course; one in which the county's single-family zoning could be sustained while awarding damages (partial compensation) to the owners of the lots at the intersection that would in some rough manner recognize the long odds against residential development.

One more example of a "tough" case: in the northwestern suburban fringe of Chicago, adjacent to one of the branches of the tollway, a shrewd developer acquired sixty acres of land surrounding a twenty-acre borrow pit. A very attractive lake was made from the pit and fifty-three single-family homes, ranging in value from $35,000 to $50,000, were built around it. By covenant, the enjoyment of the lake is reserved exclusively for the occupants of the subdivision. The only significant area of the subdivision which has remained vacant are those lots immediately adjacent to the right-of-way of the toll road. Now the developer proposes to erect multiple-family dwellings on these lots, thereby increasing the density four times what it would be if the single-family character were maintained. The arguments on both sides are appealing. The developer argues that a buyer will not invest in a 10,000 square foot single-family lot which has a high-speed limited access highway at its rear lot line; a person may, however, be willing to rent under such circumstances, knowing his investment can be terminated on a yearly basis. The assumption that home buyers in suburbs have kids while occupants of apartments generally do not may fortify this judgment. A single-family classification, the developer alleges, means that these lots will be dedicated, without compensation, as open space for the benefit of the residents of single-family homes in the subdivision.

The retort of the occupants of the detached dwelling is not confined to the customary and frequently unpersuasive remarks on the impact of multiple dwellings on single-family residence values and on the schools. In this instance the residents point, rather convincingly, to the twenty-acre lake which, with its recreational facilities, motivated them to buy. If the remaining lots are permitted to be developed at four times the density of other portions of the subdivision, the impact on this prime and limited facility will destroy its value to all. They also note that the only vehicular access to the vacant acreage is through the single-family area and the presumed additional traffic resulting from additional residential units will not be in the best interests of the present community.

Here is a case where the judge is frustrated because the present technique for resolving zoning disputes is inadequate. If the local government succeeds in protecting the existing residents it will probably postpone indefinitely the developer's opportunity to obtain a fair return on his investment in the balance of his property. If, on the other hand, the developer succeeds, his proposal probably will frustrate the reasonable expectations of those who already bought. There is a great appeal in a method whereby these expectations would be protected but with some compensation to the developer, representing the difference between the value of the property at density 1 and its value at density 4.

The patent difficulties of valuation and appraisal are not more difficult in these instances than in cases of condemnation where the taking involves something less than the fee. There may be room for debate whether the cost should be a general obligation or should result in some form of special assessment to the properties deemed to have benefited by the restriction. This issue of the extent of the benefit is present in traditional special assessment procedures. More difficulty surrounds the future use of the land; the permanence or impermanence of the decree. There is something distasteful about a permanent restraint that limits the use of land to one purpose. Yet it is equally disconcerting to acknowledge that a subsequent legislative body may be induced to allow the developer or his successor to proceed with the precise use which he was paid to forego. Again, this difficulty exists in varying degrees in condemnation when less than a fee is taken. There is the other side of the coin. The developer having received compensation for a supposed inability to market for single-family use may, contrary to expectations, sell the lots for single-family homes the next year. The presumption would be that he sold the lots at a depressed price that was made up by the subsidy he received because of the lower market appeal of these infirm locations.

This difficulty does not, I reiterate, appear in all zoning cases. It would require a combination of a real and present public interest in maintenance of the status quo with a showing that the consequence to the owner is of a different caste from that normally deriving from any restriction on land use; i.e., loss of a chance to make more money on the property.

This condition is, however, present in more than a few cases and it underlies much of the judicial ambivalence toward this technique. The cash award by a state administrative agency may be a rough method for balancing cost and benefit but it has proved to be politically and socially acceptable in the equally difficult areas of condemnation and negligence.

There is appeal to such an administrative system. Apart from the opportunity it presents to move the debate over land use up from the narrow and frequently irrational level of landowner versus municipality, it also makes sense to relieve the courts of the intolerable task of passing upon substantive planning decisions where the bench has neither the inclination, the staff, nor the time to make such decisions.

If such a statewide body were constructed along the lines of other state or federal administrative bodies, it would not be limited solely to the passive role of waiting for disputes to come to it. It could perform an invaluable service to landowners and municipalities through a general rule-making power within the statutory framework to suggest guidelines for planning policy at local and metropolitan levels. Because it would be a single body from whose decision appeal to the *appellate* courts would be available, its errors or peccadilloes would be subject to more effective judicial scrutiny than those of two or three hundred municipal bodies. Because the agency would tend to think in terms of the entire metropolis or the state, its sanctions would inevitably impel an atmosphere of municipal decision-making with an horizon broader than the municipal boundaries.

Apart from the resistance to such a reform on substantive

grounds—the destruction of local power to set land-use policy—the protests against such a course would center upon the cost of the system and the traditional resistance to one more administrative agency. One wonders whether the resulting costs to any interested party would be as great as they are under the present system where interminable local hearings are followed by one or two rounds in court. I wager that the developer who, after half-a-dozen local hearings under our present system, has reluctantly elected to go along with local demands (in spite of legal advice that he probably could win in court), would support a system which promises greater speed in decision-making. The mortgage lending community and the title guarantee companies (reluctantly being pushed into expressing opinions on zoning) should welcome some central agency which could enforce minimum statutory standards for record keeping. All concerned with land-use regulation have a direct interest in an administrative system that will bring to it the same standardization of practice that we have come to expect in commercial law.

The above techniques, administrative and legislative, are variations on the same theme: the structure of our planning and zoning legislation after forty years needs major surgery through legislation which will regulate in greater detail procedural practices at the local level; which will speak on matters of substance where the state believes a delineation is essential between those things essentially local and those matters where regional interests must be weighed; which will delegate review of local procedure and policy to a single state-wide administrative agency.

It should be noted that nowhere does this program require that there be regional government as an administrative device. (Brashness is not the same as madness.) Local decision-making is not taken away from local government. What is changed are the legislative standards, the frame of reference, both procedural and substantive, by which the validity of these local decisions is judged so that the now silent interests may be heard, and so that these disputes may be reviewed openly, fairly, and without undue delay.

future

THE PRESSURES FOR REFORM

In spite of the pervading restlessness with our present system of land-use regulation, the increasing political power of the suburban municipalities suggests that it will require great persuasion or a substantial threat to the present system of absolute municipal control before the state legislatures will be willing to elevate the horizon of "general welfare" in land-use regulation.

The persuasion will come, as might be expected, from the federal government. Most of us are aware that Uncle Sam has taken a great interest in municipal planning during the last decade. Many of us are less conscious of the change in emphasis of this federal interest in the last two or three years, a change that has already come about in a few categories and can be expected to manifest itself on a massive scale during the next ten years.

I refer to the federal government's apparent determination that the amount of federal money available for municipal planning shall be determined by the degree to which those programs are consistent with metropolitan interests. In his 1965 State of the Union speech, President Johnson said:

> The first step [in the national effort to make the American city a better place to live] is to break old patterns—to begin to think, work and plan for the development of entire metropolitan areas.

> New and existing programs will be open to those cities which work together to develop unified long-range policies for metropolitan areas.

There have already been hints that the federal government senses that coordination in planning among local agencies should be a prerequisite to federal aid to that planning.

This emphasis has been apparent in the so-called 701 program of planning aid to municipalities where a bonus is available if the municipality is in an area where there is an on-going metropolitan planning process. The present program of federal grants-in-aid for open space acquisition calls for submission of the proposed acquisition to an agency concerned with metropolitan planning. The Federal Highway Act prohibits approval by the Bureau of Roads after July 1, 1965, of any federal-aided highway project in an urban area unless such project is based on a "continuing, comprehensive transportation planning process carried on cooperatively by the state and the locality." The new Department of Housing and Urban Development has an Assistant Secretary in charge of metropolitan planning.

These illustrations are only that part of the iceberg above water. The federal government has two-score programs covering grants for local services—for urban renewal, hospitals, airports, sewage disposal, air and water pollution, to name only a handful. It can be expected that the availability of federal funds will be determined by the extent to which municipalities have coordinated their programs with those of their neighbors.

We will soon witness the end of strictly bilateral negotiations between Uncle Sam and the municipal applicant in these and other areas. It is evident that the federal government is persuaded that it can by the traditional cash carrot compel our proliferating local governments to adopt a less parochial view of physical and economic planning. The flow of grants will be measured by the togetherness of the separate municipalities in each metropolitan area.

I do not regard it as outrageous that our local petitions for federal money to help build such inter-municipal services as hospitals, sewers, highways, and airports, should be subject to the comments of a metropolitan agency that may have a sensitivity to the interests of the entire metropolis, the residents of which did, after all, contribute in part that cash we reach for. It passes reason that some people believe that municipalities can ask for outside financial help and still expect that they may use those funds as pleases them only. If each region does not take the responsibility to evaluate the regional consequences of local proposals for federally aided local projects, it is certain the federal government itself is going to do so. The issue is not whether the federal government shall contribute to the financing of municipal planning. That question, it seems to me, has already been answered. The issue today is whether the regulation which is an inevitable consequence of Uncle Sam's largess shall be tempered by the voice of the region in which those federal gifts are distributed.

If the carrot to induce a reappraisal of the municipal-metropolitan relationship is the contingency of federal subsidies, the stick is with the courts. Washington may induce a sensitivity to the metropolitan impact of municipal decision-making; the state courts are in a position to insist upon it, and to stimulate a revision of the state enabling legislation.

The threat will be felt when the courts question the assumption that underpins the traditional interpretation of land-use statutes and ordinances; namely, that each corporate municipality, regardless of size, shape, or lack of responsibility for public services, is the repository of the general welfare. Were the courts in zoning disputes to permit the introduction of evidence of the regional impact of suburban decisions over density of development, for example, this would lead to judicial questioning of the holiness of these decisions. This inquiry, in turn, would inevitably lead to judicial disapproval of many local restrictions, not, by the way, because of a compassion for the developer but because the traditional municipal reasons for restricting the landowner may be irrelevant or contrary to the real "general welfare" in an interdependent metropolitan society. When the courts reappraise the premises underlying municipal zoning law and threaten to shake the "presumption of validity" of the acts of each local legislature in cases where those municipal acts are inconsistent with the larger "community," then will each municipality reluctantly consent to statutory criteria that recognize the legitimate interests of the region. Threatened with a substantial loss of control over local land-development policy by judicial action, then the municipalities will accept a really comprehensive redefinition of general welfare as a basis for land-use regulation.

If this sounds like a plea for untidy judicial activism one answer is that such an aggressive judicial role is in the mainstream of

American law. In the charged areas of school desegregation and legislative reapportionment, the state legislatures did not act until the courts were persuaded to revise their own views and thereby confront the states with chaos. The law of land-use control has an emotional temperature only a few degrees less heated than that found in those two public issues.

I believe there is a chance that the courts will reappraise the legal basis for equating the "general welfare" with the interests of each municipality. The judge is as sensitive as the next person to economic and social demands and he is, I suspect, less inhibited than his brother in the legislature in responding to those demands. The more perceptive judges will respond to the pressures to break down those barriers to efficient public services and social mobility now represented by the zoning practices of hundreds of municipalities in our metropolitan areas. The more restrictive become the local practices, the more difficult it will be for the bench to avoid asking whether each village can define the general welfare in its own image, irrespective of the public costs.

One can, of course, find isolated zoning cases where the courts have appeared to recognize the appropriateness of intermunicipal considerations. In some of these cases, however, the only issue was whether the separation of neighboring properties by a municipal boundary line foreclosed invocation of the usual zoning criterion: character of the neighborhood.

> The appellant spells out from the language of these constitutional and statutory provisions that the responsibility of a municipality for zoning halts at the municipal boundary lines without regard to the effect of its zoning ordinances on adjoining and nearby land outside the municipality. Such a view might prevail where there are large undeveloped areas at the borders of two contiguous towns, but it connot be tolerated where, as here, the area is built up and one cannot tell when one is passing from one borough to another. Knickerbocker Road and Massachusetts Avenue are not Chinese walls separating Dumont from the adjoining boroughs. At the very least Dumont owes a duty to hear any residents and taxpayers of adjoining municipalities who may be adversely affected by proposed

zoning changes and to give as much consideration to their rights as they would to those of residents and taxpayers of Dumont. To do less would be to make a fetish out of invisible municipal boundary lines and a mockery of the principles of zoning.[4]

This sounds like a call for metropolitan standards, but the issue was whether one municipality could ignore neighboring residential development that happened to be in another municipality. This is not a great advance for metropolitanism; it merely assures that political boundaries will not prevent the invocation of neighborism.

The other class of cases where the words of the opinion suggest a repudiation of the equation of general welfare with the municipality results, ironically, in just the reverse. Here speaks the United States Court of Appeals on the powers of Valley View, Ohio:

> Traditional concepts of zoning envision a municipality as a self-contained community with its own residential, business and industrial areas. It is obvious that Valley View, Ohio, on the periphery of a large metropolitan center, is not such a self-contained community, but only an adventitious fragment of the economic and social whole. We cannot conclude as a matter of law that an ordinance which places all of the area of such a village into a residential district is *per se* arbitrary and unreasonable, with no substantial relation to the public health, safety, morals or general welfare. . . . The council of such a village should not be required to shut its eyes to the pattern of community life beyond the borders of the village itself.[5]

One wonders whether the same court would require the "council of such a village" to *open* its eyes "to the pattern of community life" beyond its borders.

The same metropolitan focus appears in the much-cited *Duffcon Concrete Products* case:

> What may be the most appropriate use of any particular property depends not only on all the conditions, physical, economic and social, prevailing within the municipality and its needs, present and reasonably prospective, but also on the nature of the entire region in which the municipality is located and the use to which the land in that region has been or may be put most advantageously. The

effective development of a region should not and cannot be made to depend upon the adventitious location of municipal boundaries, often prescribed decades or even centuries ago, and based in many instances on considerations of geography, of commerce, or of politics that are no longer significant with respect to zoning. The direction of growth of residential areas on the one hand and of industrial concentration on the other refuses to be governed by such artificial lines. Changes in methods of transportation as well as in living conditions have served only to accentuate the unreality in dealing with zoning problems on the basis of the territorial limits of a municipality, improved highways and new transportation facilities have made possible the concentration of industry at places best suited to its development to a degree not contemplated in the earlier stages of zoning.[6]

Here the court was sustaining the right of a municipality to exclude absolutely industrial plants from its boundaries.

This is a favorite ploy of municipalities when invoking regional or metropolitan considerations to justify exclusionary policies. Thus, in the much quoted *Lionshead Lake* case,[7] the New Jersey borough, defending the requirement that every one-story building must have not less than 768 square feet of floor space, put into the record evidence that within Passau County there were, indeed, places where people could build smaller houses. Why this line of argument?

First to show that there are a number of towns that don't have any zoning at all, which surround Wayne Township, for the purpose of indicating that there is no scarcity of places for people to go who want to build houses of any size.[8]

Another example of the use of the technique of citing "available" areas in the region to justify exclusion of an unwanted use involved the Wiltwyck School for Boys. This institution provided a home and school for delinquent boys in upstate New York in cooperation with New York City Welfare and Correctional Agency. It sought to relocate nearer to New York City and bought property in Yorktown, a suburb up the Hudson. It should not have surprised Wiltwyck that Yorktown forthwith passed an amendment to its zoning ordinance, the intent of which was to exclude such an institution from Yorktown. Yorktown was the third municipality to react in such a fashion. The school decided it might as well fight this one and it eventually won on the theory that it was only a "school" and "schools" were permitted.[9] The significance of this case for our purposes is that, as in the *Lionshead Lake* case, the town argued, through a professional planner-witness, that there were plenty of other villages that did not prohibit such uses and hence the region, if not Yorktown, had made adequate provision for such a use.

I suppose this technique might be called "the law of fortuitous availability" or be dubbed "unconscious regionalism." Whatever it is labelled, it is about time some court hoist such communities by their own petard and suggest that two can play at the game of regional or metropolitan considerations.

We are told by some writers that:

> [t]he use of regionalism to uphold legislative action is one thing, to strike it down quite another. It may be unrealistic for the land planner to adhere to political as opposed to social and economic boundaries, but New Jersey's constitution-makers and its legislators have placed the zoning power on the municipal level.[10]

I wonder. To vest decision-making in municipalities does not mean that they can regulate without regard for the "general welfare," and under our system a court still retains the power to reinterpret that resilient phrase.

Admittedly, there is little, if any, hard evidence of such a change in judicial attitudes. Neither was there significant evidence that the United States Supreme Court was going to reverse absolutely in 1954 the "separate but equal facilities" doctrine. Even less was there a basis for predicting that same court's response in the case of legislative reapportionment. The clues to those cases lay not in the Supreme Court's prior opinions but in the accumulated political demands for a change in the rules in order to keep the existing social revolution within the frame of the democratic process. One cannot find clues to change in judicial attitudes on land-use policy by searching the opinions. The basis for prediction rests on the evident changes in our way of living and in our urban interdependence, and the confluence of these social and economic pressures with the self-interest of an important segment of the business community, the builder and his suppliers.

There are a few hints from the courts themselves. One might infer that something is in the air from recent actions of supreme courts in a few states, actions designed to relieve themselves of the trivia of most zoning litigation, yet to retain the right of review, as the Illinois court said, in zoning cases of "state-wide significance." If the top appellate courts no longer see most zoning cases as an interminable series of petty disputes over whether a house or a gas station should be at the corner, they may begin to probe the implications of major land-use debates.

In the cases themselves, the best, if not the only, hint of a new direction is in a dissenting opinion. (The articulate dissent has an established role in American jurisprudence as a forecast of things to come.)

The dissent of Justice Frederick Hall of the New Jersey Supreme Court in *Vickers v. Township of Gloucester*,[11] should be required reading for every planning student and every member of a municipal plan commission or legislature. The majority of the New Jersey Supreme Court held that a rural township, twenty-three square miles in area, could validly exclude all trailer parks from its boundaries. The majority observed: "If through foresight a municipality is able to anticipate the adverse effects of particular uses and its resulting actions are reasonable, it should be permitted to develop without the burdens of such uses."

Few judicial expressions contain so many unexamined assumptions. Is it "foresight" or luck? What are the "adverse effects" of trailer parks? In what context is the reasonableness of the municipality's "resulting actions" to be judged?

Judge Hall, who cannot be described as unfriendly to municipal planning, noted at the beginning of his dissent that the trailer park was "a symbol" of a more fundamental issue: the absolute right of municipalities to erect "exclusionary walls on their boundaries." For our purposes, however, it is Judge Hall's challenge to the traditional role of the judiciary in land-use disputes that is significant. He noted that the majority opinion was grounded on the presumption of the validity of municipal action, and on the requirement that the proof by the landowner overcame that presumption beyond debate. The majority, he says, applies these principles in a perfunctory manner, allowing the judicial process to go far off the mark.

> Proper judicial review to me can be nothing less than an objective, realistic consideration of the setting—the evils or conditions sought to be remedied, a full and comparative appraisal of the public interest involved and the private rights affected, both from the local and broader aspects, and a thorough weighing of all factors, with government entitled to win if the scales are at least balanced or even a little less so.

Under the majority's interpretation of the general welfare, Judge Hall observed, it is hard to conceive of any local action which would *not* be debatable.

> Certainly general welfare does not automatically mean whatever the municipality says it does, regardless of who is hurt and how much. . . . The . . . general welfare transcends the artificial limits of political subdivisions and cannot embrace merely narrow local desires.

If Justice Hall's opinion had been the majority view, it would be fair to predict that the mood among municipal decision-makers in New Jersey would have been close to panic. After the first shock had worn off it is likely that the cooler heads would have suggested that all municipalities must approach the problem of trailer camps—and other pariahs of land development—as an inter-municipal problem and not as a contest between municipalities to see who could avoid being the last to exclude and hence the most vulnerable to attack. There might then have followed negotiations leading to a regional policy on appropriate locations and standards for trailer parks and to a more sensible approach to tax policy on trailers. That policy would be a compromise between the wishes and fears of each of the municipal participants hammered out in an awareness that in the absence of an agreement they would hang separately. In such a way a judicial indictment of the practice of a single township could lead to a broader base for planning. The court could not plan for the region but it could compel regional criteria as the only alternative to total loss of control over the particular development.

The same judicial protest, probably in a dissent at first, can be expected in the area of apartment development in the suburbs. One of these days some judge in a jurisdiction that has encountered the population explosion is going to take a second look at the bases on which suburban governments exclude or narrowly limit multiple-family development. He is going to reflect on the chasm between the old clichés about tenements and the facts of modern design of residential buildings. As he listens to the customary municipal pleas not to permit the destruction of the "character" of the neighborhood, he will start to ask why, in fact, detached dwellings and attached dwellings cannot live side by side. And this troublesome line of inquiry may lead him to reflect on other values which may be impaired by the policies of low density and uniform type that are under attack. Can the municipality insist on maintaining half-acre lots even if the consequence is leapfrogging of development into the outer fringes of suburbia with higher costs to the county or state in road-building and public transportation? As the state governments increase their share of local school costs, and the federal government undertakes financial aid to schools, the judge may regard with increased skepticism the plea of the municipality that apartments overburden the schools. The judge may even be tempted to suggest that if the census predictions are reasonably accurate and an additional two million persons will be living in the particular metropolis in 1970, it is not consistent with the general welfare that each municipality with available open land should be making independent decisions on the where and how much of that growth without the slightest regard for the rest of the metropolis.

This chain of thought could lead to a startling conclusion: the "character" the village cherishes is less deserving a value than the "character" of the metropolis in ten years, and that any rational basis for rejecting the developer's proposal, if it is to be rejected, must include an appraisal of the costs and benefits his proposal brings to the greater "community" of which the village is only a small part.

As I look back over these pages I am haunted by the sense of trying to run with the fox and chase with the hounds. Am I linked with the good guys or the bad? My distaste for the judicial arithmetic that equates each municipality with general welfare is equalled by my boredom with talk of metropolitan government.

The players in this game have, I hope, my understanding if not always my sympathy. The suburban resident will eventually lose out in his struggle, if not by the illogic of his legal and social position, then by the seduction of federal funds that extract a metropolitan price. The builder will find himself on every side with an inexplicable array of friends and enemies, depending on the demands of the market place. The planner will find some way to extract himself from his professional ambiguity—at a price—and he will, by inventing a subclass of technicians, throw the zoning monster off his shoulders.

For the judge we can only hope that he will, by some heroic advance in administrative techniques, be relieved of the tedium that zoning represents today, and so be made aware of those seminal issues in land regulation disputes that now are sunk by the mass of trivia.

What can be said for the attorney? As much as the bar as a whole has ignored zoning or treated it as an annoyance, it is the lawyer who invented this device and it probably will be the job of the lawyer to rescue zoning from its dismal state.

The rules are less capable of summary. In my judgment, social influences, far more than economic considerations, motivate the public decision-makers in zoning matters. Cost is not as important as status.

The path of reform of the substantive chaos in land-use law, if any is to be achieved, leads to the bench before it can emerge from the legislature. The uncertain political balance in the state legislatures permits no reform in this area in the absence of a substantial challenge by the courts to current practices. The current swing to one-man, one-vote in the state legislatures will only increase the power of the suburbs which have the most to lose from legislative reform in zoning law.

The legislative job is to reform, without delay, the incredible disarray of zoning procedure and—when stung by the courts—to command new and less parochial standards by which the reasonableness of municipal decisions will be tested.

Finally—and this comment I hope will not be forgotten—I believe that public regulation of private use of land is worth reforming—saving, if you please. This will be a blow to those who believe they find in this work only the jeers of the pamphleteer. There is little evidence in the history of land development in America that the private decision-maker, left to his own devices, can be trusted to act in the public interest. And there's the rub. Today, the measure of public interest employed to limit private decision-making is warped.

Notes and Index

Notes

Brief List of Books Cited

Bassett, Edward M. *Zoning: The Laws, Administration and Court Decisions During the First Twenty Years*. New York: The Russell Sage Foundation, 1936.

Bettman, Alfred. *City and Regional Planning Papers*. Cambridge, Mass.: Harvard University Press, 1946.

Delafons, John. *Land-Use Controls in the United States*. Cambridge, Mass.: Joint Center for Urban Studies of the Massachusetts Institute of Technology and Harvard University, 1962.

Jacobs, Jane. *The Death and Life of Great American Cities*. New York: Random House, 1961.

Mace, Ruth L. (ed.). *Cost-Revenue Research in the United States . . . 1933–1960*. Chapel Hill: Institute of Government, University of North Carolina, 1961.

Mumford, Lewis. *The City in History*. New York: Harcourt, Brace & World, [1961].

Wood, Robert C. *1400 Governments: The Political Economy of the New York Metropolitan Region*. With Vladimir V. Almendinger. Cambridge, Mass.: Harvard University Press, 1961.

Introduction

1. The term "municipal" is employed in its broadest sense to include any political subdivision of a state (city, village, town, or county) that has been given the power to zone. The reader will find few references to that handmaiden of zoning, subdivision control. This omission is not because subdivision regulation is unimportant in directing land development. It clearly is. Zoning, however, has been characterized by a high degree of public participation and judicial surveillance that are not so evident in the case of subdivision regulations.

189

2. The reader should be advised at the start that this is not an exposé of classical corruption in the zoning business. There is in zoning as in other areas of municipal government, plenty of venality. Once that has been said there is little to add that could not be said with equal fervor about streets, sewers, driveway permits, or liquor licenses. This book tries to focus on the unique characteristics of the remarkable zoning techniques, and bribery is not one of them.

Chapter I

1. Delafons, *Land-Use Controls in the United States,* p. 23.

2. Ernst Freund, "Some Inadequately Discussed Problems of the Law of City Planning and Zoning," 24 *Ill.L.Rev.* 135, 146 (1929).

3. 272 U.S. 365 (1926). The following quotations from that decision appear on pages 388 and 394–95 of the Court's opinion.

4. Bettman, *City and Regional Planning Papers,* p. 171.

5. Jesse Dukeminier Jr., "Boards of Adjustment: The Problem Reexamined," 14 *Zoning Digest* 361, 364 (1962).

6. Frederick H. Bair, "Is Zoning a Mistake?" 14 *Zoning Digest* 249 (1962).

7. Morris v. Postma, 196 A.2d 792, 796 (N.J. 1964).

8. Walter Blucher, "Is Zoning Wagging the Dog?" *Planning,* 1955 (selected papers from the Annual Planning Conference of the American Society of Planning Officials), p. 96.

9. 96 N.E.2d 731 (N.Y. 1951). The quotations that follow from this decision appear on pages 732, 736, and 738.

10. Andrew J. Dallstream and Robert S. Hunt, "Variations, Exceptions and Special Uses," 1954 *U.Ill.L.F.* 213, 236.

11. This quotation is from the tape of a conversation with Mr. Pomeroy at his office in White Plains, New York, in June, 1961. Throughout the remainder of this book excerpts will be used from this interview with Mr. Pomeroy and other interviews with planners, lay officials, and lawyers. These excerpts will not be footnoted for source, place, or date.

12. Frederick H. Bair, "Zoning—A Mad Tea Party," 12 *Zoning Digest* 33 (1960).

13. William B. Munro, "A Danger Spot in the Zoning Movement," 155 *Annals of the American Academy of Political and Social Science,* 202, 203 (1931).

14. From the Foreword to Home Title Guaranty Company, *Pitfalls of Zoning, A Guide for Attorneys* (1959).

Chapter II

1. Morris County Land Improvement Co. v. Township of Parsippany-Troy Hills, 193 A.2d 232, 239 (N.J. 1963).

2. Oregon, Ill., *Republican Reporter,* September 14, 1961. The county commission voted not to adopt the ordinance in 1961. Three years later Ogle County did finally adopt a modified version of the 1961 draft by a narrow margin. This took some courage because the campaign against the ordinance included many personal and political threats.

3. Rexford Tugwell, "The Real Estate Dilemma," 2 *Pub.Admin.Rev.* 27–40 (1945).

4. In 1965 Texas adopted a statute permitting Houston to sue to enjoin future violations of private covenants, contained in subdivision plats. Vernon's Annotated Civil Statutes, Art. 974a-1 §§ 1–3 (1965).

5. *The Rye Chronicle,* Vol. 57, No. 27, p.1 (September 5, 1963).

6. Jarrott v. Scrivener, 225 F.Supp. 827, 834 (D.C., D.C. 1964).

7. Richard F. Babcock and Fred P. Bosselman, "Suburban Zoning and the Apartment Boom," 111 *U.Pa.L.Rev.* 1040 (1963).

8. *New York Times,* August 27, 1963.

9. Wood, *1400 Governments,* pp. 93–94.

10. Ward v. Village of Skokie, 186 N.E.2d 529 (Ill. 1962). The excerpts that follow are taken from the transcript of record in that case.

11. *In Re* Diamond's Appeal, 196 A.2d 363, 369 (Pa. 1964).

12. Bettman, *City and Regional Planning Papers,* p. 27.

Chapter III

1. *House and Home,* Vol. 23, No. 1 (January, 1963), p. 115.

2. Editors of *Fortune, The Exploding Metropolis* (New York: Doubleday, 1958), p. 116.

3. Robert Seaver, "The Albatross of Localism," *House and Home,* Vol. 24, No. 6 (December, 1963), pp. 99–203.

4. Dennis O'Harrow, "Who Shot the Albatross," 30 *ASPO Newsletter* 17 (1964).

5. Raymond M. Urquhart, *A Survey of Local Government Restrictions Affecting Home Building in New York State* (a pamphlet prepared for New York State Home Builders Association, Inc. [1963?]), p. 24.

6. *Ibid.,* p.7.

7. Chicago and North Western Railroad Co. v. City of Des Plaines, Docket No. 59 C 4765, Circuit Court of Cook County, Illinois. Transcript pp. 2700–1 (1962).

Chapter IV

1. Delafons, *Land-Use Controls in the United States,* p. 95.
2. City of Ann Arbor, Michigan v. Northwestern Park Construction Corporation, 280 F.2d 212 (C.A. 6th 1960). The excerpts that follow are taken from the transcript on appeal in this case.
3. Fuller v. County Commissioners of Baltimore County, No. 235, 169–72 Transcript of Record (Oct. 1956).
4. Pearce v. Village of Edina, 118 N.W.2d 659 (Minn. 1962). The quotations that follow are taken from pages 666, 667, and 668.
5. *Journal of the American Institute of Architects,* Oct. 1961, p. 63.
6. Mumford, *The City in History,* p. 197.
7. Richard Ratcliff, *Real Estate Analysis* (New York: McGraw-Hill, 1961), p. 94.
8. 48 *Ill. Bar Journal* 930 (1960).
9. Harbison v. City of Buffalo, 152 N.E.2d 42, 51, 53 (N.Y. 1958).
10. Valley Hills Civic Ass'n v. Board of Adjustment of Tredyffrin Township, 200 A.2d 408, 413n (Pa. 1964).
11. See p. 66 et seq.

Chapter V

1. Delafons, *Land-Use Controls in the United States,* p. 23.
2. John A. McCarty, "Zoning and the Property Rights of Others," 48 *Mass.L.Q.* 473, 499–500 (1963).
3. Paul Black, "Administrative Procedure—The Stepchild of Zoning," 4 *Current Municipal Problems* 102 (1963).
4. David Craig, "Particularized Zoning: Alterations While You Wait," Southwest Legal Foundation, Institute on Planning and Zoning, *Annual Proceedings, 1960,* 1: 153, 159.
5. Robert Michalski, "Zoning—The National Peril," *Planning,* 1963. (selected papers from the Annual Planning Conference of the American Society of Planning Officials), pp. 62, 64.
6. For a description of this system see Victor Gruen, *The Heart of Our Cities* (New York: Simon & Schuster, 1964), p. 105.
7. A.L.A. Schlechter Poultry Corp. v. United States, 295 U.S. 495 (1935).
8. Anstine v. Zoning Board of Adjustment of York Township, 190 A.2d 712 (Pa. 1963).
9. Rezler v. Village of Riverside, 190 N.E.2d 706 (Ill. 1963).
10. Midland Electric Coal Corporation v. Knox County, 115 N.E.2d 275 (Ill. 1953).
11. International Harvester Co. v. Board of Appeals of the City of

Chicago, 193 N.E.2d 856 (Ill. App. 1963).

12. State *ex. rel.* Saveland Park Holding Corp. v. Wieland, 69 N.W.2d 217 (Wis. 1955).

13. Reid v. Architectural Board of Review of the City of Cleveland Heights, 192 N.E.2d 74 (Ohio App. 1963).

Chapter VI

1. Board of Adjustment of the City of Harrisburg v. Bomgardner, 195 A.2d 356, 358–59 (Pa. 1963).

2. *In Re* Heidorn's Appeal, 195 A.2d 349, 352 (Pa. 1963).

3. Vulcan Materials Company v. Griffith, 114 S.E.2d 29, 31–32 (Ga. 1960).

4. McCarthy v. City of Manhattan Beach, 264 P.2d 932 (Cal. 1953).

5. Consolidated Rock Products Co. v. City of Los Angeles, 370 P.2d 342 (Cal. 1962); *app. dis.* 371 U.S. 36 (1962).

6. *The Washington Star,* December 1, 1963.

7. First National Bank of Evanston v. City of Evanston, 197 N.E.2d 705 (Ill. 1964); Tidewater Oil Company v. Mayor and Council of the Borough of Carteret, 209 A.2d 105 (N.J. 1965).

8. Ward v. Village of Skokie, 186 N.E.2d 529, 533 (Ill. 1962).

9. Tireman-Joy-Chicago Improvement Ass'n v. Chernick, 105 N.W.2d 57, 58 (Mich. 1960).

10. Maughan v. Davis Investment Co., 184 N.E.2d 538, 539 (Ohio App. 1961).

11. Jacobson v. Preston Forest Shopping Center, Inc., 359 S.W.2d 156, 160 (Tex. Civ. App. 1962).

12. Village of Euclid, Ohio v. Ambler Realty Co., 297 Fed. 307, 316 (N.D. Ohio, 1924); *rev'd* 272 U.S. 365 (1926). For a collection of these early cases, see Richard F. Babcock and Fred P. Bosselman. "Suburban Zoning and the Apartment Boom," 111 *U.Pa.L.Rev.* 1040–49 (1963).

13. Vickers v. Township Committee, 181 A.2d 129, 148 (N.J. 1962).

14. Nectow v. City of Cambridge, Mass., 277 U.S. 183 (1928).

15. First National Bank of Evanston v. City of Evanston, 197 N.E.2d 705, 708–9 (Ill. 1964).

Chapter VII

1. George L. Creamer, "The Social Paradox of Zoning and Land Controls in an Expanding Urban Economy," 39 *Dicta* 269, 290 (1962).

2. Ratcliff, *Real Estate Analysis,* p. 328.

3. Allison Dunham, "A Legal and Economic Basis for City Planning," 58 *Colum.L.Rev.* 650, 658–59 (1958).

4. Norman Williams, "Planning Law and Democratic Living," 20 *Law & Contemp.Prob.* 317, 334 (1955).

5. Finley Peter Dunne, "On Property Rights," in *Mr. Dooley on the Choice of Law,* ed. by Edward J. Bander (Charlotteville, Va.: Michie Co., 1963), p. 74.

6. Charles M. Haar, "In Accordance with a Comprehensive Plan," 20 *Law & Contemp.Prob.* 317, 334 (1955).

Chapter VIII

1. Rockhill v. Township of Chesterfield, 128 A.2d 473, 479 (N.J. 1962).

2. Norman Williams, "Development Controls and Planning Controls—The View from 1964," *Proceedings of the 1964 Annual Conference, American Institute of Planners,* pp. 73–74.

Chapter IX

1. Bettman, *City and Regional Planning Papers,* p. 55.

2. The material on pages 149–50 first appeared in Richard F. Babcock and Fred P. Bosselman, "Suburban Zoning and the Apartment Boom," 111 *U.Pa.L.Rev.* 1040 (1963).

Chapter X

1. Richard F. Babcock, "The Chaos of Zoning Administration," 12 *Zoning Digest* 1 (1960).

2. Strohl v. Macon County Board of Appeals, 104 N.E.2d 612 (Ill. 1952). Abstract, pp. 6–7 (Docket No. 32215).

3. Lindburg v. Zoning Board of Appeals, 133 N.E.2d 266, 268 (Ill. 1956).

4. Borough of Cresskill v. Borough of Dumont, 104 A.2d 441, 445–46 (N.J. 1954).

5. Valley View Village, Inc. v. Proffett, 221 F.2d 412, 418 (C.A. 1955).

6. Duffcon Concrete Products, Inc. v. Borough of Cresskill, 64 A.2d 347, 349 (N.J. 1949).

7. Lionshead Lake, Inc. v. Township of Wayne, 10 N.J. 165, 89 A.2d 693 (N.J. 1952): *app. dis.* 344 U.S. 919 (1953).

8. Val Nolan, Jr., and Frank E. Horack, Jr., "How Small a House?

—Zoning for Minimum Space Requirements," 67 *Harv.L.Rev.* 967, 984 (1954).

9. Wiltwyck School for Boys, Inc. v. Perry, 182 N.E.2d 268 (N.Y. 1962). There is an excellent discussion of this interesting case in 71 *Yale L.J.* 720 (1962).

10. Note 8, *supra* at pp. 984–85.

11. 181 A.2d 129 (N.J. 1962). The quotes that follow from that opinion appear on pages 138, 144, 145, and 146.

Index